A Lot Of Little Fires

"*Wherefore glorify ye the Lord in the fires, even the name of the Lord God of Israel in the isles of the sea.*"
—Isaiah 24:15 KJV

David L. Martin

Publishing assistance by BookCrafters, Parker, Colorado.
www.bookcrafters.net

Dedication

SINCE THIS IS MY FIRST attempt at a writing project there are many people I would like to dedicate it to. But for obvious reasons I will stick with the short list.

First of all, without the inspiration from our Lord Jesus Christ it would have never happened. To my parents, Herbert and Juanita Martin who did their best to train me up in the way I should go. Also my wife Tracy who has lived with me long enough she should know this book means much to me.

My three beautiful daughters, Tara, Jana, and Kari (who conceived & designed the cover!) are my heroes in the faith!

And a special dedication to my friend (my only friend besides Jesus-private joke) Pastor Randy Langford who has went on to be with the Lord. And finally, to a group of godly men, pastors, mentors, sometimes tormentors, leaders, and examples. Rev. James G. Riggs, Bruce Thompson, Bishop Randy Adams, Rev. Kevin Shindoll and Pastor Jimmy Toney.

Foreword

I DON'T THINK OF MYSELF as another Dwight L. Moody, Leonard Ravenhill, David Brainerd, E.M. Bounds, or Andrew Murray. Or the multitude of other men and women who are infinitely more anointed and qualified. But I wanted to write a book about prayer.

Am I an authority on prayer? Nope. Have I seen great miracles of healing and deliverance through prayer? Some, not many. Have I witnessed supernatural manifestations of God by way of a prayer experience? Nothing anyone would call "supernatural." Have I seen thousands of souls prayed through to the Holy Ghost because of fervent effective prayer? No, in fact some would probably say that the opposite has happened in my ministry.

But prayer and what it can do according to the Word of God has always held a fascination for me. I believe in the power and practice of prayer. But I am in no way considered a prayer warrior.

The idea for this book then came as a result of Pastoring a church in Lawrenceburg, Tennessee for about 8 ½ years. In our church as in many I suppose, prayer has to a certain degree "lost its savor." (So, to speak). And so, I decided as Pastor to dedicate one of our three regular services to focus on or emphasize prayer.

From that 4-5 year journey I learned much about prayer. And the result is what is contained in these pages. Some are relatively short, because I always wanted to use the majority of time in prayer, but some are longer lessons that I also used on Wednesday night Bible Study. Also included is a two multi-part series on prayer interspersed throughout the other chapters.

If nothing else, the time I spent in study and practice of the prayer principles that were learned made me more aware of the presence of God. And I still long for more!

Regardless of what I consider a lack of powerful personal experience, my desire is that you will glean something from these pages that will help you in your Christian experience in prayer!

—David L. Martin

Table of Contents

Introduction
Principles of Flesh & Spirit

Everything that is spirit must pass through the flesh.

Everything that is invisible must pass through the visible.

Everything that is supernatural must pass through the natural.

Everything that is spiritual must pass through the physical.

Everything that requires spiritual understanding must pass through the human brain.

Every spiritual principle requires human faith and action.

The plan of God is spiritual but requires human interaction.

The promises of God are spiritual but without human acceptance they are of none affect.

The gifts of the Spirit are obviously spiritual, but can only be manifested in a committed human life.

The fruit of the Spirit is spiritual but again requires human action & expression.

Worship is spiritual but requires human knees to bow in submission.

Praise is spiritual but in order for it to draw the presence of God it requires human hands to clap, human voices to sing & shout, human legs to dance.

Prayer is spiritual but requires human lips and tongue and voice to speak with human expression and understanding.

Faith is spiritual but requires human trust and obedience.

Fasting is spiritual but requires human flesh to refrain from eating physical food.

Salvation is spiritual ... but required a physical sacrifice.

Repentance is spiritual but requires the human brain and will to turn away from sin.

Baptism is spiritual but requires human flesh to be buried in water.

The Word of God is spiritual but it required that the Word of God to become flesh and dwell among us.

God is a spirit but he required of himself to come in human form and flesh and to shed human blood and experience human suffering.

So that means that the Spirit of God is looking for, searching for, seeking for a willing human vessel to move through.

Chapter 1

A House of Prayer

Matthew 21:11-13

(11) And the multitude said, "This is Jesus the prophet of Nazareth of Galilee."

(12) And Jesus went into the temple of God, and cast out all them that sold and bought in the temple, and overthrew the tables of the moneychangers, and the seats of them that sold doves,

(13) And said unto them, "It is written, My house shall be called the house of prayer; but ye have made it a den of thieves."

Isaiah 56:4-7

(4) "For thus saith the LORD unto the eunuchs that keep my sabbaths, and choose the things that please me, and take hold of my covenant;

(5) Even unto them will I give in mine house and within my walls a place and a name better than of sons and of daughters: I will give them an everlasting name, that shall not be cut off.

(6) Also the sons of the stranger, that join themselves to the LORD, to serve him, and to love the name of the LORD, to be his servants, every one that keepeth the sabbath from polluting it, and taketh hold of my covenant;

(7) Even them will I bring to my holy mountain, and make them joyful in my house of prayer: their burnt offerings and their

*sacrifices shall be accepted upon mine altar; for mine house shall be called **an house of prayer** for all people".*

A PRAYER PRINCIPLE ...

God was not speaking of an earthly "house" or a physical structure that we have come to call "church." God teaches and illustrates through many ways so that we can understand spiritual truths through physical examples. In my personal experience these are defined by what one of my former Pastors, James Riggs, called "types and shadows."

The "house of prayer" that both Isaiah and Matthew wrote about, (under the inspiration of the Holy Ghost), was not solely in reference to a physical structure. I know in Matthew's gospel Jesus is standing in the temple in Jerusalem. But He is using that physical reference point to illustrate the real nature of His desire.

God doesn't need a house, a temple or a tabernacle. But He does want a place where He can exercise intimate communication with mankind. The whole matter of salvation isn't just to save us from our sins, it is also God's ultimate desire is to make our mortal bodies, these earthen vessels, these tabernacles of flesh into more than a place where He visits two or three times a week, but a place where there is constant intimate fellowship, praise, worship and yes ... prayer within US.

Here are three scriptures to illustrate ...

1 Corinthians 3:16-17 KJV ... *(16) "Know ye not that ye are the temple of God, and that the Spirit of God dwelleth in you?*

(17) If any man defile the temple of God, him shall God destroy; for the temple of God is holy, which temple ye are."

1 Corinthians 6:19-20 KJV ... *(19) "What? know ye not that your*

body is the temple of the Holy Ghost which is in you, which ye have of God, and ye are not your own?

(20) For ye are bought with a price: therefore glorify God in your body, and in your spirit, which are God's."

1 Peter 2:5 KJV ... *"Ye also, as lively stones, are built up a spiritual house, an holy priesthood, to offer up spiritual sacrifices, acceptable to God by Jesus Christ."*

What follows is what I shared with the church that I was privileged to Pastor when I began to feel the burden to focus on prayer ...

"This morning I toyed with the idea of dismissing the young people and having prayer, especially if we had no visitors. And having prayer in every service until we see a move of God in our church and in our city."

The burden I felt for prayer on that day was almost overwhelming. But it describes what every born-again believer should experience, but let's move on.

Maybe I'm being too narrow minded here, but in our text, Jesus isn't talking about a house of worship or praise. And He's not talking about a house of preaching or teaching. Or anything else that the Church should actively be engaged in.

But He describes His "house" as the house of prayer. What some of us in this modern-day church don't realize is this. Without prayer, everything else is without power or anointing. Preaching and teaching without prayer is all but ineffective.

Worship, praise, singing and playing without prayer is just entertainment. Outreach events without prayer are simply another event in the community.

5

Prayer was and is meant to be the power and anointing before and behind everything we do. Without prayer we're just another group of people who come together 3 times a week. Without prayer, no matter how well prepared and eloquently presented preaching affects the very few. Without prayer there are no healings, no miracles, and no revival. Without prayer there are no new births, no transformation from sin, and no deliverance from the power of the enemy.

MAYBE IT'S BECAUSE WE DON'T KNOW WHAT REAL PRAYER IS ...

The word "prayer" in at least the Isaiah's prophecy is from another root word in the Hebrew that means to intercede or to intervene.

To intercede ... *"to act or interpose in behalf of someone in difficulty or trouble."*

To intervene ... *"to come between disputing people, groups, etc.; intercede; mediate. Also... "to occur incidentally so as to modify or hinder:,"* And finally ... *"to interfere with force or a threat of force."*

PRAYER WAS NEVER MEANT TO BE SOMETHING BENIGN OR PASSIVE.

We live in a day which lacks spiritual intervention and intercession. This generation has a desire to pray but not the will to pray. We want to pray but don't have the will to execute it. We are like the disciples in the garden...

Matt. 26:40-41

(40) "And he cometh unto the disciples, and findeth them asleep, and saith unto Peter, What, could ye not watch with me one hour?

(41) Watch and pray, that ye enter not into temptation: the spirit indeed is willing, but the flesh is weak."

They had the desire to pray because they had seen the results of the prayers of Jesus. They knew that pray was important, perhaps even vital, but they didn't have the will to execute it. We must consciously decide to engage in both intercession and intervention.

The desire to pray isn't enough. We must have the will to pray. Our weaknesses and failures are because we don't realize the cost of true prayer. And the will to pray isn't something we ask God to provide. He either can't, won't or both. It must be born out of a burning desire within us!

GOD CANNOT GIVE US THE WILL TO PRAY...

Prayer is the foundation for everything we do. Without it we are helpless and hopeless. We must engage our human will in prayer to activate the spiritual power of God.

If our earthly vessels are to become a true house of prayer, a true house of intervention, a true house of intercession, we must make this declaration within ourselves and perhaps even say it out loud ...

Not just that I want to pray, not just that I need to pray, but that I WILL PRAY!

Chapter 2

"Before Every Great Revival..."

Acts 8:1-13 ... *(1) "And Saul was consenting unto his death. And at that time there was a great persecution against the church which was at Jerusalem; and they were all scattered abroad throughout the regions of Judaea and Samaria, except the apostles.*

(2) And devout men carried Stephen to his burial, and made great lamentation over him.

(3) As for Saul, he made havock of the church, entering into every house, and haling men and women committed them to prison.

(4) Therefore they that were scattered abroad went every where preaching the word.

(5) Then Philip went down to the city of Samaria, and preached Christ unto them.

(6) And the people with one accord gave heed unto those things which Philip spake, hearing and seeing the miracles which he did.

(7) For unclean spirits, crying with loud voice, came out of many that were possessed with them: and many taken with palsies, and that were lame, were healed.

(8) And there was great joy in that city.

(9) But there was a certain man, called Simon, which beforetime in the same city used sorcery, and bewitched the people of Samaria, giving out that himself was some great one:

(10) To whom they all gave heed, from the least to the greatest, saying, This man is the great power of God.

(11) And to him they had regard, because that of long time he had bewitched them with sorceries.

(12) But when they believed Philip preaching the things concerning the kingdom of God, and the name of Jesus Christ, they were baptized, both men and women.

(13) Then Simon himself believed also: and when he was baptized, he continued with Philip, and wondered, beholding the miracles and signs which were done."

2 Cor. 2:11 ... *"Lest Satan should get an advantage of us: for we are not ignorant of his devices."*

Most of us have at some point been in a great revival service. Many of us have seen, heard and felt the power and presence of God. But I don't think any of us have ever experienced a great revival. During times of great revival according to both the Bible and historical record, revival is preceded by these things in some form.

1.) A heightened sense or hunger for God.

2.) Consistent prayer and fasting.

3.) Repentance and seeking God.

4.) But the one thing that we don't anticipate is ...
   opposition from the enemy!

Paul said to the Church in II Cor. 2:11 that we shouldn't be ignorant of Satan's devices.

Or put another way, his strategies or methods. Opposition from the enemy can take on many forms and come from any direction. He knows that once God begins to pour out His Spirit there is little he can do to hinder it. But that never stops him from trying. He is committed to destroying, disrupting, and dividing God's people so the effect of revival will allow him to make God's move the least it can be.

9

So, we must recognize Satan when he tries to kill, steal, and destroy the revival that God has promised the Church. It's not enough to know that Satan right now is trying to sow fear in every heart of every believer. We need to act, we need to stand, we need to be faithful even when we face opposition.

Before every great revival there is spiritual blindness, spiritual ignorance, and spiritual opposition. We can't fight the last one until we realize we're under the influence of the first two.

We as God's people must be aware that without prayer, fasting and repentance we are spiritually blind and ignorant. While we are in that condition Satan doesn't have to do much. But when our eyes begin to open and our understanding is enlightened, Satan has no choice but to directly oppose the Work of God.

Just some of the examples of God allowing His people to face opposition ...

- In Egypt, Pharoah's heart was hardened and opposed the release of God's people.

- At the mountain of God, they were opposed by the enemy with the worship of Golden calf, Korah and his rebellious friends, and Moses was even opposed by his own sister Miriam. (Family is a biggie)

- In Neh. 4 God's people were trying to rebuild the walls of Jerusalem but they were opposed by Tobiah and Sanballat.

- Ammonites, Moabites, Jebusites, Amorites, Perizzites, Midianites, Philistines, etc.

- In Daniel chapter 10 it reads ...

Daniel 10:1-14 ... *(1) "In the third year of Cyrus king of Persia a thing was revealed unto Daniel, whose name was called Belteshazzar; and the thing was true, but the time appointed was long: and he understood the thing, and had understanding of the vision.*

(2) In those days I Daniel was mourning three full weeks.

(3) I ate no pleasant bread, neither came flesh nor wine in my mouth, neither did I anoint myself at all, till three whole weeks were fulfilled.

(4) And in the four and twentieth day of the first month, as I was by the side of the great river, which is Hiddekel;

(5) Then I lifted up mine eyes, and looked, and behold a certain man clothed in linen, whose loins were girded with fine gold of Uphaz:

(6) His body also was like the beryl, and his face as the appearance of lightning, and his eyes as lamps of fire, and his arms and his feet like in colour to polished brass, and the voice of his words like the voice of a multitude.

(7) And I Daniel alone saw the vision: for the men that were with me saw not the vision; but a great quaking fell upon them, so that they fled to hide themselves.

(8) Therefore I was left alone, and saw this great vision, and there remained no strength in me: for my comeliness was turned in me into corruption, and I retained no strength.

(9) Yet heard I the voice of his words: and when I heard the voice of his words, then was I in a deep sleep on my face, and my face toward the ground.

(10) And, behold, an hand touched me, which set me upon my knees and upon the palms of my hands.

(11) And he said unto me, O Daniel, a man greatly beloved, understand the words that I speak unto thee, and stand upright: for unto thee am I now sent. And when he had spoken this word unto me, I stood trembling.

(12) Then said he unto me, Fear not, Daniel: for from the first day that thou didst set thine heart to understand, and to chasten thyself before thy God, thy words were heard, and I am come for thy words.

(13) But the prince of the kingdom of Persia withstood me one

and twenty days: but, lo, Michael, one of the chief princes, came to help me; and I remained there with the kings of Persia.

(14) Now I am come to make thee understand what shall befall thy people in the latter days: for yet the vision is for many days."

The first thing that Daniel's spoken prayer produced was ... opposition! It wasn't revelation, it wasn't authority, it wasn't healing or miracles or deliverance. It was the essential ingredient to every move of God whether personal or public ... good old-fashioned opposition!

In Acts 13:8 ...

"But Elymas the sorcerer (for so is his name by interpretation) <u>withstood them</u>, seeking to turn away the deputy from the faith."

God uses any and every method to accomplish His purpose. Even opposition from friend and foe alike. Opposition doesn't always come from the devil or evil. Opposition doesn't always come from the fearful and unbelieving. Opposition may come from friends and family. Opposition may even come from God Himself! (I guess that's where the gift of discerning of spirits comes in.) Nevertheless, no matter what or who the source of opposition comes from, God uses opposition to temper us. To make us stronger, to make us more powerful in Him, and make us more effective for the Kingdom of God.

WHEN REVIVAL COMES TO THIS GENERATION...

THERE WILL BE OPPOSITION!

- *Opposition in our families*
- *Opposition in our jobs*
- *Opposition in our church*
- *Opposition against everything we do for the kingdom no matter how great or small.*
- *SO, OPPOSITION IN ITSELF SHOULD BE A SIGN THAT REVIVAL IS CLOSE!*

10 Things Satan Can't Do
—Jennifer Hereen – Crosswalk.com

1.) *Satan can't make me sin*

2.) *Satan can't make me fear death.*

3.) *Satan can't take my energy, stamina, or joy.*

4.) *Satan can't pester me after I resist*

5.) *Satan can't control me.*

6.) *Satan can't be everywhere at once*

7.) *Satan can't do anything without God's permission*

8.) *Satan can't steal my faith.*

9.) *Satan can't command or control my future.*

10.) *Satan can't win!*

Chapter 3

Behind the Ephod

1 Samuel 21:1-15

(1) "Then came David to Nob to Ahimelech the priest: and Ahimelech was afraid at the meeting of David, and said unto him, Why art thou alone, and no man with thee?

(2) And David said unto Ahimelech the priest, The king hath commanded me a business, and hath said unto me, Let no man know any thing of the business whereabout I send thee, and what I have commanded thee: and I have appointed my servants to such and such a place.

(3) Now therefore what is under thine hand? give me five loaves of bread in mine hand, or what there is present.

(4) And the priest answered David, and said, There is no common bread under mine hand, but there is hallowed bread; if the young men have kept themselves at least from women.

(5) And David answered the priest, and said unto him, Of a truth women have been kept from us about these three days, since I came out, and the vessels of the young men are holy, and the bread is in a manner common, yea, though it were sanctified this day in the vessel.

(6) So the priest gave him hallowed bread: for there was no bread there but the shewbread, that was taken from before the LORD, to put hot bread in the day when it was taken away.

(7) Now a certain man of the servants of Saul was there that day,

detained before the LORD; and his name was Doeg, an Edomite, the chiefest of the herdmen that belonged to Saul.

(8) And David said unto Ahimelech, And is there not here under thine hand spear or sword? for I have neither brought my sword nor my weapons with me, because the king's business required haste.

(9) **And the priest said, The sword of Goliath the Philistine, whom thou slewest in the valley of Elah, behold, it is here wrapped in a cloth behind the ephod: if thou wilt take that, take it: for there is no other save that here. And David said, There is none like that; give it me.**

(10) And David arose, and fled that day for fear of Saul, and went to Achish the king of Gath.

(11) And the servants of Achish said unto him, Is not this David the king of the land? did they not sing one to another of him in dances, saying, Saul hath slain his thousands, and David his ten thousands?

(12) And David laid up these words in his heart, and was sore afraid of Achish the king of Gath.

(13) And he changed his behaviour before them, and feigned himself mad in their hands, and scrabbled on the doors of the gate, and let his spittle fall down upon his beard.

(14) Then said Achish unto his servants, Lo, ye see the man is mad: wherefore then have ye brought him to me?

(15) Have I need of mad men, that ye have brought this fellow to play the mad man in my presence? shall this fellow come into my house?"

THERE'S NO "I" IN "WE"

Or

THERE'S NO "WE" IN "I"

You know like there's no "I" in team, kind of thing. (Michael Jordan & the Chicago Bulls) When we use the term "we," we are referring to the church as a whole. One for all, and all for one. But in that "we," there are "I's" or individuals that make up the "we."

The question from this point in revival isn't what are "we" are going to do, but what am "I" going to do? The question isn't what have "we" learned in this revival, but what have "I" learned? The question isn't what will "we" do differently now to move the kingdom forward, but what will "I" do differently now to move the kingdom forward?

THE MAIN THING IS ...

That we (I mean, "I") act on the principles of faith and the Word of God. And there is no substitute for prayer and fasting. Fasting breaks the power of the carnal flesh and unclean human desires and prayer connects us with the Spirit of God who has the power and the authority to do anything we pray for.

So, borrowing from the story of king David in I Sam. Chapter 21 David is ...

- *No longer a shepherd boy.*
- *He is a young warrior who has seen battle against the Philistines.*
- *He is also associated to King Saul as armor bearer & musician.*
- *Saul is rejected by God and David is anointed to be king in his place.*
- *But his time to rule has not come to pass yet.*
- *In fact, he is on the run from Saul, hiding out in caves with other fugitives and discontents.*

- *The future king of Israel is uncertain, perhaps fearful, being one step from death. Trying to figure out how to fulfill the promises that God has given him and how to proceed.*

Then he goes to Ahimilech, the priest and asks this question ... *"And is there not here under thine hand spear or sword?"*

He was perhaps thinking that he could fight his way out of his situation if he only had a weapon. Isn't it within every one of us to pursue a physical solution to every situation first? (Ouch!) And David as much as he is a positive spiritual role mode, he was no different...

And the priest answered him, *"The sword of Goliath the Philistine, whom thou slewest in the valley of Elah, behold, it is here wrapped in a cloth behind the ephod: if thou wilt take that, take it: for there is no other save that here. And David said, There is none like that; give it me."*

"LET'S FACE IT, SWORDS ARE COOL!"

(In I Samuel 17 it gives no description of the sword other than David uses it to cut off Goliath's head. – no size or weight comparison like his spear)

It must have seemed natural to a young warrior to reach first for a sword. According to one website the sword is a symbol of war, destruction, power, authority, and divine judgements. But the sword in this instance perhaps represents a carnal or human solution. (I know that we consider the sword as a symbol of the Word of God.)

But the priest reached past the Ephod (which is the symbol of prayer and direct communication with God) and gave David the sword of Goliath. But what David should have grabbed first was the Ephod. I know hindsight is pretty powerful! But the principle is there. Prayer should be the first thing we reach for in any situation.

According to jewishvirtuallibrary.org the ephod ...

Was one of three ways that God's people communicated directly with God in early Israel. There were dreams, prophets, and the Urim (lights) & the Thummim (perfection) contained in the Ephod. It was also called the Breastplate of Decision.

Some additional scripture references to the Ephod and the Urim & the Thummim ...

Exodus 28:30 KJV ... *"And thou shalt put in the breastplate of judgment the Urim and the Thummim; and they shall be upon Aaron's heart, when he goeth in before the LORD: and Aaron shall bear the judgment of the children of Israel upon his heart before the LORD continually."*

Leviticus 8:8 KJV ... *"And he put the breastplate upon him: also he put in the breastplate the Urim and the Thummim."*

Ezra 2:63 KJV ... *"And the Tirshatha (governor) said unto them, that they should not eat of the most holy things, till there stood up a priest with Urim and with Thummim."*

I Samuel 23:9 NKJV ... *"When David knew that Saul plotted evil against him, he said to Abiathar the priest, "Bring the ephod here."*

I Samuel 30:7-8 NKJV ... (7) *"Then David said to Abiathar the priest, Ahimelech's son, "Please bring the ephod here to me." And Abiathar brought the ephod to David.*

(8) So David inquired of the LORD, saying, "Shall I pursue this troop? Shall I overtake them?" And He answered him, "Pursue, for you shall surely overtake them and without fail recover all."

So, the Ephod was an O.T. type and shadow of N.T. prayer. Biblestudytools.com says this...

"God will speak directly to individuals who seek him."

WHAT IS THE PRINCIPLE?

Before we reach behind the ephod for ...

What may seem natural...

What may seem powerful...

What may seem like a good idea,...

Reach for the ephod, seek God directly in prayer!

God does use human men and women with human methods, human abilities and human actions, human frailty, and human failure, but our first priority must be prayer!

The ephod of itself probably had no direct appeal to David's humanity. I mean let's compare a piece of cloth or clothing to a sword!

But if you are in need of answers, if you need direction, if you need to hear the truth, if you need divine intervention... don't look for a human solution, seek his face!

2 Chron. 7:14 ... *"If my people, which are called by my name, shall humble themselves, and pray, and seek my face, and turn from their wicked ways; then will I hear from heaven, and will forgive their sin, and will heal their land."*

Chapter 4

The Power of Words

Part I

Psalm 5:1-3...

> *[[To the chief Musician upon Nehiloth, A Psalm of David.]]*
>
> *(1) "Give ear to my words, O LORD, consider my meditation.*
>
> *(2) Hearken unto the voice of my cry, my King, and my God: for unto thee will I pray.*
>
> *(3) My voice shalt thou hear in the morning, O LORD; in the morning will I direct my prayer unto thee, and will look up."*

IF WE ONLY KNEW HOW POWERFUL WE ARE ...

If we are human, then we all have been given a very powerful weapon. Words are one of the most powerful things God created. It was by His Words that He created everything and if we are created in His image than we have been endowed with at the very least the type and shadow of that power.

From www.inc.com ... 26 Quotes About the Power of Words

8. *"Handle them carefully, for words have more power than atom bombs."* -Pearl Strachan Hurd

9. *"Words have energy and power with the ability to help, to heal, to hinder, to hurt, to harm, to humiliate, and to humble."* -Yehuda Berg

16. "*Don't ever diminish the power of words. Words move hearts and hearts move limbs.*" -Hamza Yusuf

17. "*Words are seeds that do more than blow around. They land in our hearts and not the ground. Be careful what you plant and careful what you say. You might have to eat what you planted one day.*" -Unknown

23. "*No matter what anybody tells you, words and ideas can change the world.*" -John Keating

26. "*If we understood the power of our thoughts, we would guard them more closely. If we understood the awesome power of our words, we would prefer silence to almost anything negative. In our thoughts and words, we create our own weaknesses and our own strengths. Our limitations and joys begin in our hearts. We can always replace negative with positive.*" -Betty Eadie

These secular authors and writers confirm what the scripture says ...

Deut. 1:34 ... "*And the LORD heard <u>the voice of your words</u>, and was wroth, and sware, saying,*"

Deut. 5:28 ... "*And the LORD heard <u>the voice of your words</u>, when ye spake unto me; and the LORD said unto me, <u>I have heard the voice of the words of this people</u>, which they have spoken unto thee: they have well said all that they have spoken.*"

Deut. 29:19 ... "*And it come to pass, <u>when he heareth the words of this curse</u>, that he bless himself in his heart, saying, I shall have peace, though I walk in the imagination of mine heart, to add drunkenness to thirst:*"

Deut. 31:30 ... "*And Moses spake in the ears of all the congregation of Israel <u>the words of this song</u>, until they were ended.*"

Deut. 32:1-4 ... (1) "*Give ear, O ye heavens, <u>and I will speak; and hear, O earth, the words of my mouth</u>.*

(2) My doctrine shall drop as the rain, my speech shall distil as the dew, as the small rain upon the tender herb, and as the showers upon the grass:

(3) *Because I will publish the name of the LORD: ascribe ye greatness unto our God.*

(4) *He is the Rock, his work is perfect: for all his ways are judgment: a God of truth and without iniquity, just and right is he."*

And for 48 more verses he sings his words ... Pretty extreme for a guy who says he's "slow of speech." (It's like the "American Pie" song by Don McLean)

Job 4:4 ... "*Thy words have upholden him that was falling, and thou hast strengthened the feeble knees."*

Job 19:2 ... "*How long will ye vex my soul, and break me in pieces with words?"*

Psalm 19:14 ... "*Let the words of my mouth, and the meditation of my heart, be acceptable in thy sight, O LORD, my strength, and my redeemer."*

Psalm 54:2 ... "*Hear my prayer, O God; give ear to the words of my mouth."*

Prov. 18:4 ... "*The words of a man's mouth are as deep waters, and the wellspring of wisdom as a flowing brook."*

Prov. 18:8 ... "*The words of a talebearer are as wounds, and they go down into the innermost parts of the belly."*

Prov. 25:11 ... "*A word fitly spoken is like apples of gold in pictures of silver."*

Ecc. 8:4 ... "*Where the word of a king is, there is power: and who may say unto him, What doest thou?"*

Dan. 10:12 ... (KJV) "*Then said he unto me, Fear not, Daniel: for from the first day that thou didst set thine heart to understand, and to chasten thyself before thy God, thy words were heard, and I am come for thy words."*

Amplified Bible ... "*your words were heard, and I have come in consequence of your words."*

New Living Translation ... *"your request has been heard in heaven. I have come in answer to your prayer."*

NET ... *"your words were heard. I have come in response to your words."*

HERE IS THE POWER OF WORDS ...

Words spoken by a human tongue both good or bad have a direct influence on the environment. Both physically and spiritually. Prayer is the spoken expression of a human heart and mind. If prayer is words spoken into the atmosphere, your prayers spoken out loud have a powerful affect both on earth and in heaven.

I have heard that some people say, "Don't pray out loud because the devil can hear you and he will try to hinder your prayer". And I say, "SO WHAT!" If we are kings and priests unto God, if we have dominion on this earth, if we are submitted to Him, then our "words", our prayers have power, and therefore also have the authority to cause him or any other evil power to flee. If God is moved by your words, then every other force both good or evil is subject to your words also!

Prov. 18:21 ... *"Death and life are in the power of the tongue: and they that love it shall eat the fruit thereof."*

SO, RELEASE YOUR POWER! ...

Eze 37:1-10 ... (1) *"The hand of the LORD was upon me, and carried me out in the spirit of the LORD, and set me down in the midst of the valley which was full of bones,*

(2) And caused me to pass by them round about: and, behold, there were very many in the open valley; and, lo, they were very dry.

(3) And he said unto me, Son of man, can these bones live? And I answered, O Lord GOD, thou knowest.

(4) Again he said unto me, Prophesy upon these bones, and say unto them, O ye dry bones, hear the word of the LORD.

(5) Thus saith the Lord GOD unto these bones; Behold, I will cause breath to enter into you, and ye shall live:

(6) And I will lay sinews upon you, and will bring up flesh upon you, and cover you with skin, and put breath in you, and ye shall live; and ye shall know that I am the LORD.

(7) So I prophesied as I was commanded: and as I prophesied, there was a noise, and behold a shaking, and the bones came together, bone to his bone.

(8) And when I beheld, lo, the sinews and the flesh came up upon them, and the skin covered them above: but there was no breath in them.

(9) Then said he unto me, Prophesy unto the wind, prophesy, son of man, and say to the wind, Thus saith the Lord GOD; Come from the four winds, O breath, and breathe upon these slain, that they may live.

(10) So I prophesied as he commanded me, and the breath came into them, and they lived, and stood up upon their feet, an exceeding great army."

Matt. 8:8 ... *"The centurion answered and said, Lord, I am not worthy that thou shouldest come under my roof: but speak the word only, and my servant shall be healed."*

MY PERSONAL PERSPECTIVE ON
PREACHING & PRAYER HAS CHANGED ...
The power of words is not in the thinking of them, or in the reading of them, or in the writing of them, but in the speaking of them. SPOKEN HUMAN WORDS HAVE POWER. PERIOD. Whether meant for evil or for good. EVERY human word spoken affects the environment, and every dimension.

PREACHING & PRAYER ...

I used to think preaching was the product of someone with natural ability taking a thought and expounding on it spontaneously... without any form, you know just open your mouth and God speaks through you. (That happens very seldom.)

Sis. Vesta Mangun of Alexandria, LA. writes out her messages and then practically preaches / teaches them verbatim. At a preaching conference right in the middle of her message she turned around to someone and said something like ...

"If it was anointed when I wrote it, then it will be anointed when I preach it." (Paraphrased)

And as far as prayer is concerned, I again initially thought prayer had to be spontaneous, from the heart, off the cuff, etc.

And even some believe that you should only pray in the Spirit, i.e. praying in tongues all the time. (There is a time and season for everything) But not everyone does that either. (In fact, I would be skeptical of someone like that) The critical thing is that you are speaking out loud! In the end God isn't concerned with HOW much you speak with the gift of tongues, which is different than receiving the gift of the Holy Ghost speaking in tongues, (although I wish I spoke in tongues more than you all. HA.) But it's your voice He wants to hear! If He chooses to change your language in prayer that's His choice not yours!

I have reluctantly come to the point of this revelation. My prayers do not have to necessarily be spontaneous in origin, but they do have to be audible. The sound of my voice is what heaven and hell will hear, it is my voice which looses or binds things. It's my voice that releases my faith in God's power. It's my voice that sets the enemy to flight and releases the will of God, not my thoughts!

So, let's read this prayer out loud!

From the book ...*Prayers That Shake Heaven and Earth* ... By Daniel Duval

Morning Prayer

Father, I come before you in the mighty name of Jesus Christ. You are great, and greatly to be praised! I come boldly before your throne of grace to find mercy and grace to help in the time of need. In the morning, O LORD, you will hear my voice. In the morning, I will order my prayer to you and eagerly watch. I take this opportunity to put up smoke screens in the spirit that act as sight and sound barriers against interlopers, satanic agents, and evil spirits.

I decree that I am cleansed of all the filthiness of the flesh and spirit, perfecting holiness in the fear of the Lord. I am washed by the blood of Jesus, which cleanses me of all unrighteousness. I am washed by the water of your Word.

I decree that every evil word that was spoken over me in my dreams, evil prayers, other realms where I was taken, or that were imported into me through technologies, are now being devoured by the locusts of God loosed to create crop failure.

I declare that all evil devices, chains of bondage, evil injections, imprisonments of my humanity, insertions and implants of every type of physical, spiritual and energetic that were established against me in my sleep, are now being consumed in the holy fire of Jesus Christ. I renounce and declare destruction upon all evil altars set up bearing my name or image in every timeline, age, realm, and dimension. I renounce and break the power of all sacrifices or rituals performed on these altars, declaring that they will have no impact on me or anyone else.

I repent for and renounce every act of agreement with evil agendas and assignments taking place during my sleep, including the reception of evil spirit food, counterfeit gifts, callings, mandates, judgments, technologies, counterfeit revelations, and assignments.

I declare that the blood of Jesus covers not only my house, car(s), bank account(s), and everything under my stewardship, in Jesus name.

I declare that my body is blessed, my soul is blessed, and my spirit is blessed in Jesus name.

I call for the anointing to be poured over every component of my person, anointing me for service, establishing my heart in joy, and awakening the strength of Jesus Christ in my members.

Angels, bless the Lord and praise his holy name! You excel in strength; you perform his Word and you hearken unto the voice of his Word. You are made ministering spirits to the heirs of salvation. As an heir of salvation, I speak that your ministry to me is the execution of your assignments.

Angels of finance, you are loosed to bring me what has been appointed to my storehouse. Establish me in the provision of the Lord and cause the abundant blessings of God to overtake me.

Angels of opportunity, you are loosed to find and secure opportunities, and to establish an environment of favor around me.

Angels of healing, you are loosed to ensure that attacks against my health are derailed. You are loosed to block the transmission of infectious diseases, to prevent food poisoning, to interrupt accidents that would cause harm to my body, and to heal issues in my flesh, soul, and spirit.

Angels of warfare, you are loosed to conquest the enemies of God that oppose me in my assignments, mandates, and callings. I declare that you conquer all time thieves in the name of Jesus. I identify the strongholds, strategic positions, war rooms, and laboratories of darkness that have been erected against my life and declare that the warhorses of heaven are loosed against them. I bombard the enemy with hailstones, coals of fire, tsunamis of living water, engines of war, instruments of war, and the armies of heaven. I declare the enemy is pummeled by the smoke from the nostrils of God, the hiss of the Lord that brings bees and flies, the ravenous beasts, and light of His glory. I release the spear of the Lord, instruments of death, and the razor of the Lord by which the enemies of God are shamed. I cover the encampments of evil with clouds of confusion and smite evil realms pitted against me with plague and disaster in the name of Jesus.

I declare that the sun, moon, stars, and planets are created to praise the Lord. The earnest expectation of creation itself also will be delivered from the bondage of corruption into the glorious liberty of the children of God. Therefore, I speak to every evil assignment invested into the sun, moon, stars and planets by witches, warlocks, and the agents of darkness. I declare that they are now being excised by the sword of the Lord. I declare that these evil assignments are being replaced by the word of the Lord which says, Father in heaven, hallowed be your name, and your will be done on earth as it is in heaven.

Just as the stars fought in the courses against Sisera, I determine that the stars are now employed in exploits against the enemies of Jesus Christ and fight alongside the children of light to expand the influence of the government of God in the earth.

I declare that creation is reoriented at the outset of this day to serve the Lord and that cosmological powers are employed in the revelation of the glory of God, for it is written that the knowledge of the glory of the Lord shall cove the earth as the waters cover the sea.

I declare that the whirlwind of the Lord surrounds me and my associates. It draws unto us all resources that are expedient relative to our callings and mandates, and it destroys the snares of the enemy from before our face.

Lord Jesus, you are my shield, my buckler, and my rearguard. I take opportunity to assume the armor of God: the helmet of salvation, the breastplate of righteousness, the belt of truth, I put on the shoes of the preparation of the gospel of peace, I take up the shield of faith, the sword of the Spirit, which is the Word of God, the garments of vengeance the cloak of zeal. I will not be afraid of the terror by night, neither of the arrow that flies by day, neither, of the pestilence that walks in darkness, neither of the destruction that lays waste at noonday.

*I declare that the spirit of excellence rests upon me, and that those over me will seek to set me over entire realms. I declare that my realm is engaged in my assignments. *I call it charges with the name of Jesus Christ of Nazareth. * (This part was modified & shortened)*

I cause my realm and life to come into interface with the seven Spirits of God; the Spirit of the Lord, the Spirit of Wisdom and Understanding, the Spirit of Counsel and Might, the Spirt of Knowledge, and the Fear of the Lord.

I declare that I behold with open face the glory of the Lord and am changed into the same image from glory to glory, even as by the Spirit of the Lord. I seal these declarations across every realm, age, timeline, and dimension, past, present and future, to infinity. I call this day blessed, fruitful, and prosperous in the mighty name of Jesus Christ our Lord. AMEN.

Chapter 5

Changing the World

Rom. 7:14-25 ... NKJV *(14)* *"For we know that the law is spiritual, but I am carnal, sold under sin.*

(15) For what I am doing, I do not understand. For what I will to do, that I do not practice; but what I hate, that I do.

(16) If, then, I do what I will not to do, I agree with the law that it is good.

(17) But now, it is no longer I who do it, but sin that dwells in me.

(18) For I know that in me (that is, in my flesh) nothing good dwells; for to will is present with me, but how to perform what is good I do not find.

(19) For the good that I will to do, I do not do; but the evil I will not to do, that I practice.

(20) Now if I do what I will not to do, it is no longer I who do it, but sin that dwells in me.

(21) I find then a law, that evil is present with me, the one who wills to do good.

(22) For I delight in the law of God according to the inward man.

(23) But I see another law in my members, warring against the law of my mind, and bringing me into captivity to the law of sin which is in my members.

(24) O wretched man that I am! Who will deliver me from this body of death?

(25) I thank God—through Jesus Christ our Lord! So then, with

the mind I myself serve the law of God, but with the flesh the law of sin."

WE ARE BORN-AGAIN TO BE WORLD CHANGERS!

There's no doubt that the Apostle Paul was a World changer. Through his personal ministry and through his writings he literally has had a hand in changing or shaping the world for generations. And that's what God still expects from each one of His believers. And our excuse is, ... *"Well, I'm not Paul or Peter. I didn't witness Jesus walking on the water, turning water into wine or raising the dead."* (As far as I know neither did Paul.)

But the spiritual revolution that God is expecting from His church doesn't depend on Peter, James, or John. It doesn't depend on the government, or on the UPCI or any other Christian organization.

It doesn't depend on your Pastor or church leadership. And I may be misunderstood but it doesn't even depend on God Himself.

So how did Paul do it? Change his World. Could He change it today? Would he have the same impact on this last day's generation as he did on the first century church? So how did he do it?

I think partially through his letter to the church in Rome Paul reveals the most important thing about changing the world and experiencing spiritual revolution.

THE FIRST STEP IN CHANGING THE WORLD ...

In those twelve verses is the secret of Paul's success of changing the world. It's not about the power of the gospel (which is indeed the power of our salvation). It's not about the power of the Holy Ghost (which definitely provides power for the believer). It's not about Paul's eloquence or teaching ability. It's not about who he had on his ministry team. It's not about his music / praise team (if he had one). It's not about his abundance of education, knowledge or revelations.

It's all about "I." In those twelve verses of scripture the word "I" occurs 26 times. In this case it really is all about "me" or "I." (Toby Keith – "I Wanna Talk About Me!")

In other words, the whole world and everything in it comes down to one thing "me."

"I," or myself, the most important person in the world.

I don't have to change anyone else, because I can't change you, and the church can't change you, and even bringing to bear all His power and glory even God can't change you. (But He can make you miserable.) In order to change the world, I just have to change ME.

When I get "I" fixed, when get "I" willing, when I get "I" to a place of repentance and obedience, when I get "I" out of the way then the world isn't quite as big. When I get the "I" figured out, then "I" can have a spiritual revolution! When I get the "I" in line, then I can have revival. When I get the "I" subdued and die daily, the world will change!

HOW TO HAVE REVIVAL ...

One preacher said it this way ... *to have a mighty revival. Go home, turn off your phone, etc. and go to your room take something and mark a circle. Sit in that circle and seek God till revival comes.*

Why? Because revival, spiritual revolution happens one "I" at a time!

Chapter 6

Burning the Incense

Malachi 1:11

"*For from the rising of the sun even unto the going down of the same my name shall be great among the Gentiles; and in every place incense shall be offered unto my name, and a pure offering: for my name shall be great among the heathen, saith the LORD of hosts.*"

Luke 1:5-12 ... (5) "*There was in the days of Herod, the king of Judaea, a certain priest named Zacharias, of the course of Abia: and his wife was of the daughters of Aaron, and her name was Elisabeth.*

(6) And they were both righteous before God, walking in all the commandments and ordinances of the Lord blameless.

(7) And they had no child, because that Elisabeth was barren, and they both were now well stricken in years.

(8) And it came to pass, that while he executed the priest's office before God in the order of his course,

*(9) According to the custom of the priest's office, **his lot was to burn incense when he went into the temple of the Lord.***

*(10) **And the whole multitude of the people were praying without at the time of incense.(11) And there appeared unto him an angel of the Lord standing on the right side of the altar of incense**.*

(12) And when Zacharias saw him, he was troubled, and fear fell upon him.

THE TABERNACLE IS A BUNCH OF TYPES & SHADOWS ...

Contained in the rich and fertile story of the Tabernacle of the Wilderness is a wealth of types & shadows for the New Testament church. Physical examples of spiritual principles.

One of the most beautiful is what the Altar of Incense represents. The writer of Hebrews illustrates what the Tabernacle represents to the Church ...

Hebrews 9:1-5 NKJV (1) *"Then indeed, even the first covenant had ordinances of divine service and the earthly sanctuary.*

(2) For a tabernacle was prepared: the first part, in which was the lampstand, the table, and the showbread, which is called the sanctuary;

(3) and behind the second veil, the part of the tabernacle which is called the Holiest of All,

(4) which had the golden censer and the ark of the covenant overlaid on all sides with gold, in which were the golden pot that had the manna, Aaron's rod that budded, and the tablets of the covenant;

(5) and above it were the cherubim of glory overshadowing the mercy seat. Of these things we cannot now speak in detail."

And then he goes on to say ...

Hebrews 9:6-9 ... (NKJV) (6) *"Now when these things had been thus prepared, the priests always went into the first part of the tabernacle, performing the services.*

(7) But into the second part the high priest went alone once a

year, not without blood, which he offered for himself and for the people's sins committed in ignorance;

(8) the Holy Spirit indicating this, that the way into the Holiest of All was not yet made manifest while the first tabernacle was still standing.

(9) It was symbolic for the present time in which both gifts and sacrifices are offered which cannot make him who performed the service perfect in regard to the conscience;"

To the children of Israel these things were extremely REAL. If they did not perform the law as prescribed by God, they suffered either death or rejection or both. But to the N.T. believer in Christ they represent spiritual principles vital to our eternal destination.

The rituals, the sacrifices, the articles of furniture of the Tabernacle represent something greater than just physical objects, they represent spiritual principles to be directly applied to our Christian experience.

SPECIFICALLY, THE ALTAR OF INCENSE

Exodus 30:1-10 KJV ... (1) *"You shall make an altar to burn incense on; you shall make it of acacia wood.*

(2) "A cubit shall be its length and a cubit its width—it shall be square—and two cubits shall be its height. Its horns shall be of one piece with it.

(3) "And you shall overlay its top, its sides all around, and its horns with pure gold; and you shall make for it a molding of gold all around.

(4) "Two gold rings you shall make for it, under the molding on both its sides. You shall place them on its two sides, and they will be holders for the poles with which to bear it.

(5) "You shall make the poles of acacia wood, and overlay them with gold.

(6) *"And you shall put it before the veil that is before the ark of the Testimony, before the mercy seat that is over the Testimony, where I will meet with you.*

(7) *Aaron shall burn on it sweet incense every morning; when he tends the lamps, he shall burn incense on it.*

(8) *"And when Aaron lights the lamps at twilight, he shall burn incense on it, a perpetual incense before the LORD throughout your generations.*

(9) *"You shall not offer strange incense on it, or a burnt offering, or a grain offering; nor shall you pour a drink offering on it.*

(10) *"And Aaron shall make atonement upon its horns once a year with the blood of the sin offering of atonement; once a year he shall make atonement upon it throughout your generations. It is most holy to the LORD."*

LET'S LOOK AT THE SPECS ...

- *Made of shittim / acacia wood overlaid with gold – symbolizes glory & holiness*
- *The last thing before you entered the Holy of Holies -the presence of God.*
- *A place where the priest left his will and his pride.*
- *It had four horns where blood was applied for purity and cleansing. Atonement / Reconciliation*
- *It took fire to consume/ produce the sweet-smelling savour.*
- *A place of continual burning. (Renewed in the morning & evening)*
- *Wood overlaid with gold – symbolized the nature of Christ ... humanity / divinity*
- *A place of worship and praise and petition*
- *A place where things are lifted up.*

THE INCENSE THAT WAS PLACED UPON IT...

Exodus 30:34-37 KJV ... (34) "And the LORD said unto Moses, __*Take unto thee sweet spices, stacte,* and *onycha,* and *galbanum*__; these sweet spices with pure *frankincense*: of each shall there be a like weight:

(35) And thou shalt make it a perfume, a confection after the art of the apothecary, tempered together *(rubbed or washed with salted), pure and holy:*

(*__Mark 9:49-50__ ... "For every one shall be salted with fire, and every sacrifice shall be salted with salt.

(50) Salt is good: but if the salt have lost his saltness, wherewith will ye season it? Have salt in yourselves, and have peace one with another.")*

(36) And thou shalt **beat some of it very small**, and put of it before the testimony in the tabernacle of the congregation, where I will meet with thee: it shall be unto you most holy.

(37) And as for the perfume which thou shalt make, ye shall not make to yourselves according to the composition thereof: it shall be unto thee holy for the LORD.

The incense was measured, specific, unique, prepared, pure and holy.

THE INCENSE IS A TYPE & SHADOW
OF PRAYER & PRAISE ...

We don't have to burn incense anymore. But we do offer both a living sacrifice and the fruit of our lips and our tongue in prayer, praise and worship. Once again, the sweet incense in the O.T. law is described as unique, (one of a kind), exclusive to the Tabernacle, and to God a *sweet savour*. And so are the prayers and praise of His N.T. saints! There is also a reason that we no longer have need of burnt offerings and sacrifices. Jesus Christ has become our one-time all-encompassing sacrifice. What does that have to do with it and what does it have to do with the altar of incense or prayer and praise?

If we did, perhaps we would understand something about prayer and praise ...

GOD IS ATTRACTED BY THE SMELL OF DEATH

The O.T. records at least 42 times where the phrase sweet savour is listed, and in each instance, it is in direct reference to the death of an innocent animal sacrificed in atonement for sin.

But God didn't command Moses to get some sweet spices to "cover up" the smell of death. It was for the purpose of associating death with prayer and praise.

From: www.bible-history.com/tabernacle/TAB4The_Golden_Altar_of_Incense.htm

The incense was burnt on pieces of hot coal, which the priest removed in a censer or fire pan from the altar of burnt offering in the courtyard. A censer apparently was a shallow bowl or pan with a handle on it. It could also be used for removing the ashes from the altar or gathering up the burnt parts of the wick from the lampstand.

The golden altar was used for burning incense

Poured out on burning coals the incense produced a delightful aroma in the Holy Place. It was the offering of the person whose sins had been forgiven by blood and who then went on to express the fragrance of love and worship, which was most pleasing to God.

- *The common priest would burn these holy spices on the altar over 700 times in a year.*
- *The sweet incense was to be kept burning at all times. (Pray without ceasing)*

Leviticus 16:12-13 ... (12) *"And he shall take a censer full of burning coals of fire from off the altar before the LORD, and his hands full of sweet incense beaten small, and bring it within the vail:*

(13) And he shall put the incense upon the fire before the LORD, that the cloud of the incense may cover the mercy seat that is upon the testimony, that he die not:"

In other words, in order to be pleasing to God, the smell of death (N.T. repentance) was mingled with fragrant aroma of a mixture of pure spices. The spices weren't to cover up the stench of death, rather both aromas mingled together were required to make the sacrifice acceptable to God.

THAT'S WHY DAILY REPENTANCE IS SO IMPORTANT ...

Repentance is the fulfillment of that type and shadow. If you pray or offer praise to God without repentance, without the smell of death, it is strange fire.

Nadab / Abihu (Lev. 10:1)

Lev 10:1 ... *"And Nadab and Abihu, the sons of Aaron, took either of them his censer, and put fire therein, and put incense thereon, and offered strange fire before the LORD, which he commanded them not."*

But N.T. priests don't offer up dead sacrifices or burn the incense. We offer a living sacrifice and continual prayer and praise. But that living sacrifice like Paul mentions in

I Cor. 15:31 has to *die daily through repentance!*

Is Your prayer and praise acceptable to God?

Is the smell of death / repentance mingled with your prayers and praise?

Chapter 7

Encouraging Yourself

I Samuel 30:1-6

(1) "And it came to pass, when David and his men were come to Ziklag on the third day, that the Amalekites had invaded the south, and Ziklag, and smitten Ziklag, and burned it with fire;

(2) And had taken the women captives, that were therein: they slew not any, either great or small, but carried them away, and went on their way.

(3) So David and his men came to the city, and, behold, it was burned with fire; and their wives, and their sons, and their daughters, were taken captives.

(4) Then David and the people that were with him lifted up their voice and wept, until they had no more power to weep.

(5) And David's two wives were taken captives, Ahinoam the Jezreelitess, and Abigail the wife of Nabal the Carmelite.

(6) And David was greatly distressed; for the people spake of stoning him, because the soul of all the people was grieved, every man for his sons and for his daughters: but David encouraged himself in the Lord his God."

Ephesians 5:17-21

(17) "Wherefore be ye not unwise, but understanding what the will of the Lord is.

(18) And be not drunk with wine, wherein is excess; but be filled with the Spirit;

(19) Speaking to yourselves in psalms and hymns and spiritual songs, singing and making melody in your heart to the Lord;

(20) Giving thanks always for all things unto God and the Father in the name of our Lord Jesus Christ;

(21) Submitting yourselves one to another in the fear of God."

It is no mystery. We are a part of something that the world has a hard time understanding. We are described as the church, the elect, the body of Christ, the bride of Christ, the chosen of God. We are a diverse yet unified group of all kinds of people, from virtually every race, every culture and every class of humanity yet we are welded together by a like precious faith and a common obedience to God's Holy word. Yet again that body is made up of individual members, with different talents, abilities, temperaments, and passions. Without the individual members there would be no body.

It is true that we draw strength from each other, and we are to edify and build up each other each time we gather together in Jesus' name. But what about the times we are alone or outside the presence of the rest of the church? Do we maintain the joy and the faith that being in a group perhaps is easier to declare?

Of all the "heroes" of the Bible King David stands out as one of the greatest. Not because he killed a lion and a bear, not because he killed Goliath, not because he had slain his ten thousands as the people claimed, not because of all his brave exploits, and not even because he could sing and worship and touch God's heart. But because he had the desire and the ability to encourage himself.

It is obvious that the house of the Lord became a passion of David's ...

Psalm 23:6 ... *"Surely goodness and mercy shall follow me all the days of my life: and I will dwell in the house of the LORD for ever."*

Psalm 27:4 ... *"One thing have I desired of the LORD, that will I seek after; that I may dwell in the house of the LORD all the days of my life, to behold the beauty of the LORD, and to enquire in his temple."*

Psalm 92:13 ... *"Those that be planted in the house of the LORD shall flourish in the courts of our God."*

Psalm 122:1 & 9 ... *[A Song of degrees of David.] "I was glad when they said unto me, Let us go into the house of the LORD."*

(9) "Because of the house of the LORD our God I will seek thy good."

Psalm 135:1-3 ... *(1) "Praise ye the LORD. Praise ye the name of the LORD; praise him, O ye servants of the LORD.*

(2) Ye that stand in the house of the LORD, in the courts of the house of our God,

(3) Praise the LORD; for the LORD is good: sing praises unto his name; for it is pleasant."

It wasn't the location that got David excited, he never saw the temple completed. He worshipped in a tent! There wasn't any of the gold and silver and brass of Solomon's temple on display, it was the Ark of the Covenant, the presence of God that caused David to declare those things.

Imagine if you will...

In II Samuel 6 David is bringing the Ark of the Covenant home to Jerusalem...

2 Samuel 6:5 ... *"And David and all the house of Israel **played**"*

before the LORD on all manner of instruments *made of fir wood, even on harps, and on psalteries, and on timbrels, and on cornets, and on cymbals."*

2 Samuel 6:13 … *"And it was so, that when they that bare the ark of the LORD had gone six paces, he sacrificed oxen and fatlings.*

(14) And David danced before the LORD with all his might; and David was girded with a linen ephod.

(15) So David and all the house of Israel brought up the ark of the LORD with shouting, and with the sound of the trumpet."

Now I'll admit that there is something about the singing, and all those instruments that can get you pumped up. And all those sacrifices, and all those testimonies, and all the shouting. The strength and excitement of that moment would encourage almost anyone. But that's not what set David apart. David's relationship with God didn't start in the house of the Lord, it ended there. That moment was the product of many hard-fought battles, many sleepless nights seeking God, many times when I'm sure he didn't see God at work, but David had that special gift and desire …

But in our text (I Sam. 6:1-6), David is not in the middle of a parade, there is no Ark, there is no singing or shouting of praise, there aren't any instruments (if there are they're not being played), there's no sacrificing, no worship, and no Holy Ghost goose bumps…

But there was fire and smoke, devastation and destruction, missing wives and children, weeping and mourning, David was distressed, and there was talk of stoning him. There was no hey, let's have church! There wasn't any church. There wasn't even the Ark. There wasn't anyone else. At that moment David didn't even have a friend, let alone a choir!

But the secret to David's power with God is contained at the end of verse six…

"… but David encouraged himself in the Lord his God."

It was something David learned ....

...before He was a king...

...before he felt the anointing oil on his head...

... before he was a mighty warrior...

... before he killed his ten thousand's...

...before he killed Goliath...

...before he killed the Lion and the bear...

It was something he received all by himself, out in the middle of a pasture watching a flock of sheep. He sang all the solos, he prayed all by himself, he learned to seek God and worship without the fanfare and noise of a large group of people. Because He understood God's power and presence didn't depend on instruments and choirs and buildings. And when the time came to go to a central location with those of likeminded faith it just made it sweeter!

Before we go to the house of God, know this, ... We need the church, it's vital in our walk with God, but what we should need most of all is the ability to entertain the presence of God all by ourselves!

ALL BY MYSELF ...

I believe that there is a story floating out there about a missionary who encountered a young man from a remote area. And that young man probably a relatively new believer asked the missionary something like this.

"Sir, what do I do if I should get discouraged in my faith and you or another believer isn't around to pray with me?"

And the missionary said something like, "If you have the Holy Ghost, you have the same power and privilege that I do. Take your hand and place it on your head and pray! You will receive the same presence of God to help you in your discouragement!"

Encourage yourself!

Chapter 8

The Power of Words

Part II

Psalm 5:1-3 ... [[To the chief Musician upon Nehiloth (a pipe or flute plural), A Psalm of David.]] (1) *"Give ear to my words, O LORD, consider my meditation.*

(2) Hearken unto the voice of my cry, my King, and my God: for unto thee will I pray.

(3) My voice shalt thou hear in the morning, O LORD; in the morning will I direct my prayer unto thee, and will look up."

THE POWER OF PRAYING OUTLOUD ...

In part one of this study, we established that words have power. They can build up or destroy. They can define our thoughts and our dreams. They release the power of our inner man to accomplish great things or guarantee failure.

And so, if words have power, then prayers that are spoken have power. The difference between mere words spoken and prayer is that prayers are words spoken with faith. And may I point out it isn't exclusive to Christians. The founders of BLM are said to be heavily involved in social & political movements. But from several different sources they also by their own words appear to be heavily involved in the occult and witchcraft.

From a program called *The Hamilton Corner* the host of the

program reads this direct quote from one of the founders, Patrisse Cullors, which said this about their movement ...

"I'm calling for us spiritually to be radical, we're not just having a social justice movement, we are having a spiritual movement."

She goes on to say in another interview ... *"Maybe I'm sharing too much but we become very intimate with the spirits we call on regularly, right, like each of them seems to have a different presence and personality, I laugh a lot with Waukesha, you know, who I didn't meet in my body."*

And also, in that interview they speak openly about summoning the spirits of their dead ancestors. Now whether you agree with their social or political views or not, my point is this ...

They are trying very hard to accomplish their agenda with not only physical protest, intimidation and violence but having heard even a portion of that interview they are submitting and soliciting spiritual powers that are not of God. Even if they don't use the word "prayer" they are using the power of words to connect with these "spirits." In my opinion that is the same as prayer. It is simply the power of their spoken words that releases these "spirits" to operate freely through them and by their direct invitation.

IF IT WORKS FOR THEM ...

What's the matter with us? Prayer is obviously not some passive waste of time. Prayer is or should be words spoken out loud by a human being with faith, confidence, and relationship with the spiritual power to which they are speaking.

THE BIG SHOWDOWN ...

1 Kings 18:19-40 ... (19) *"Now therefore send, and gather to me all*

Israel unto mount Carmel, and the prophets of Baal four hundred and fifty, and the prophets of the groves four hundred, which eat at Jezebel's table.

(20) So Ahab sent unto all the children of Israel, and gathered the prophets together unto mount Carmel.

(21) And Elijah came unto all the people, and said, How long halt ye between two opinions? if the LORD be God, follow him: but if Baal, then follow him. And the people answered him not a word.

(22) Then said Elijah unto the people, I, even I only, remain a prophet of the LORD; but Baal's prophets are four hundred and fifty men.

(23) Let them therefore give us two bullocks; and let them choose one bullock for themselves, and cut it in pieces, and lay it on wood, and put no fire under: and I will dress the other bullock, and lay it on wood, and put no fire under:

(24) And call ye on the name of your gods, and I will call on the name of the LORD: and the God that answereth by fire, let him be God. And all the people answered and said, It is well spoken.

(25) And Elijah said unto the prophets of Baal, Choose you one bullock for yourselves, and dress it first; for ye are many; and call on the name of your gods, but put no fire under.

(26) And they took the bullock which was given them, and they dressed it, and called on the name of Baal from morning even until noon, saying, O Baal, hear us. But there was no voice, nor any that answered. And they leaped upon the altar which was made.

(27) And it came to pass at noon, that Elijah mocked them, and said, Cry aloud: for he is a god; either he is talking, or he is pursuing, or he is in a journey, or peradventure he sleepeth, and must be awaked.

(28) And they cried aloud, and cut themselves after their manner with knives and lancets, till the blood gushed out upon them.

(29) And it came to pass, when midday was past, and they prophesied until the time of the offering of the evening sacrifice,

that there was neither voice, nor any to answer, nor any that regarded.

(30) *And Elijah said unto all the people, Come near unto me. And all the people came near unto him. And he repaired the altar of the LORD that was broken down.*

(31) *And Elijah took twelve stones, according to the number of the tribes of the sons of Jacob, unto whom the word of the LORD came, saying, Israel shall be thy name:*

(32) *And with the stones he built an altar in the name of the LORD: and he made a trench about the altar, as great as would contain two measures of seed.*

(33) *And he put the wood in order, and cut the bullock in pieces, and laid him on the wood, and said, Fill four barrels with water, and pour it on the burnt sacrifice, and on the wood.*

(34) *And he said, Do it the second time. And they did it the second time. And he said, Do it the third time. And they did it the third time.*

(35) *And the water ran round about the altar; and he filled the trench also with water.*

(36) *And it came to pass at the time of the offering of the evening sacrifice, that Elijah the prophet came near, and said,* **LORD God of Abraham, Isaac, and of Israel, let it be known this day that thou art God in Israel, and that I am thy servant, and that I have done all these things at thy word.**

(37) **Hear me, O LORD, hear me, that this people may know that thou art the LORD God, and that thou hast turned their heart back again.** *(63 words brought down fire from heaven)*

(38) *Then the fire of the LORD fell, and consumed the burnt sacrifice, and the wood, and the stones, and the dust, and licked up the water that was in the trench.*

(39) *And when all the people saw it, they fell on their faces: and they said, The LORD, he is the God; the LORD, he is the God.*

(40) And Elijah said unto them, Take the prophets of Baal; let not one of them escape. And they took them: and Elijah brought them down to the brook Kishon, and slew them there."

LET'S EXPAND ON THAT ...

If the human words spoken by Elijah had the power to call down fire from heaven, then how much more powerful would it be if N.T. believers prayed the Word of God out loud? It may not happen the first time we pray but prayer is a progressive skill that we learn as we go.

From an internet article
"Praying God's Word Out Loud for a Spiritual Breakthrough"
By Debbie Przybylski

In a similar way we have a powerful weapon—the Word of God. We can kick the enemy and defeat him by speaking the Word of God. Praying the Bible out loud is powerful for spiritual breakthrough. Praying God's Word with our lips is a dangerous weapon to Satan. He knows the power of the Word of God.

Many Christians do not realize that praying the Word out loud breaks through the enemy's defenses. It can bring destruction to his plans and bring victory to God's purposes. Let's not be ignorant of the power we have in the Bible. Let's learn to use the Word of God and speak it out loud for spiritual breakthrough. When we do, the spiritual atmosphere of entire cities can change. We can make a huge impact in our neighborhoods through praying or singing God's Word out loud and over it. The government of God is released through our prayers.

THE WORD OF GOD IS FILLED WITH "PRAYERS"...

According to *lifecoach4god.life* there are at least 650 prayers recorded in our Bible. And there are at least 25 spoken by Jesus himself. So why would God allow those "words" of humanity speaking their prayers be recorded in His word if they didn't have some kind of significance or example for us?

If the Word of God is swift and powerful as a two-edged sword when we read it, why wouldn't it be as much or even more powerful when we pray it?

To briefly illustrate, in my KJV there are notes added to many of the Psalms giving reference to the content or the subject of each Psalm. (These "songs" are prayers set to music or with musical accompaniment.

Psalm 4 ... Evening Prayer for Deliverance

Psalm 5 ... Morning Prayer for Guidance

Psalm 6 ... Prayer for God's Mercy

Psalm 10 ... Petition for God's Judgment

Psalm 13 ... The Prayer for God's Answer – Now

Psalm 17 ... A Prayer of David – *"Hide me under the shadow of thy wings"*

Psalm 18 ... Thanksgiving for deliverance by God (50 verses long)

Psalm 25 ... Acrostic prayer for instruction. (22 verses – 22 letters Hebrew alphabet, each verse begins with a letter from that alphabet)

Psalm 28 ... Rejoice Because of Answered Prayer

Psalm 35 ... Petition for God's Intervention

Psalm 44 ... Prayer for Deliverance by God

Psalm 54 ... (2) *"Hear my prayer, O God; give ear to the words of my mouth."*

And there are more ...

God may be able to read your thoughts but here are a few more scriptures emphasizing the idea that God would rather hear you speak the words of your heart and mind ...

Psalm 84:8 ... *"O LORD God of hosts, hear my prayer: give ear, O God of Jacob. Selah."*

Psalm 102:1 ... [[A Prayer of the afflicted, when he is overwhelmed, and poureth out his complaint before the LORD.]] *"Hear my prayer, O LORD, and let my cry come unto thee."*

Nehemiah 1:6 ... *"Let thine ear now be attentive, and thine eyes open, that thou mayest hear the prayer of thy servant, which I pray before thee now, day and night, for the children of Israel thy servants, and confess the sins of the children of Israel, which we have sinned against thee: both I and my father's house have sinned."*

Psalm 64:1 ... [[To the chief Musician, A Psalm of David.]] *"Hear my voice, O God, in my prayer: preserve my life from fear of the enemy."*

WHY SHOULD WE USE SOMEONE ELSE'S WORDS?

Well one reason why is that for many of us, expressing our thoughts and prayers in spoken words to God isn't as easy as it sounds. If the power of human speech is universally powerful, then the power of spoken prayer with faith is even more powerful. I don't believe God is looking for originality, He wants to "hear" your voice expressing your desires and supplications. It doesn't matter to God if someone else has prayed that same prayer! It doesn't matter if you say or pray it just so, just say and pray it!

THE WORD OF GOD IS THE UNIVERSAL HUMAN EXPRESSION ...

So why wouldn't we use the most inspired, most powerful, most effective words we could speak in prayer. Which is the Word of God!

Psalm 42:1 ... [[To the chief Musician, Maschil, for the sons of Korah.]] *"As the hart panteth after the water brooks, so panteth my soul after thee, O God.*

(2) My soul thirsteth for God, for the living God: when shall I come and appear before God?

(3) My tears have been my meat day and night, while they continually say unto me, Where is thy God?

(4) When I remember these things, I pour out my soul in me: for I had gone with the multitude, I went with them to the house of God, with the voice of joy and praise, with a multitude that kept holyday.

(5) Why art thou cast down, O my soul? and why art thou disquieted in me? hope thou in God: for I shall yet praise him for the help of his countenance.

(6) O my God, my soul is cast down within me: therefore will

I remember thee from the land of Jordan, and of the Hermonites, from the hill Mizar.

(7) Deep calleth unto deep at the noise of thy waterspouts: all thy waves and thy billows are gone over me.

(8) Yet the LORD will command his lovingkindness in the daytime, and in the night his song shall be with me, and my prayer unto the God of my life."

(9) I will say unto God my rock, Why hast thou forgotten me? why go I mourning because of the oppression of the enemy?

(10) As with a sword in my bones, mine enemies reproach me; while they say daily unto me, Where is thy God?

(11) Why art thou cast down, O my soul? and why art thou disquieted within me? hope thou in God: for I shall yet praise him, who is the health of my countenance, and my God."

Hearing the Word is powerful, speaking the Word is even more powerful!

Chapter 9

Making God Bigger

Ps. 34:3 ... *"O magnify the LORD with me, and let us exalt his name together."*

Ps. 69:30 ... *"I will praise the name of God with a song, and will magnify him with thanksgiving."*

Ez. 38:23 ... *"Thus will I magnify myself, and sanctify myself; and I will be known in the eyes of many nations, and they shall know that I am the LORD."*

Usually when you hear the word "magnify" it means that you are making the object of your attention bigger so that it can be seen and understood.

Acts 10:46 ... *"For they heard them speak with tongues, and magnify God. Then answered Peter,"* (The N.T. Greek word "magnify" is translated as ...)

-    *to make conspicuous, to celebrate, to deem or declare great.*

Any time we do a word study in the Bible you must understand how and to who the word is applied. That's because not only something may be lost in translation from the original language, but some words and their translations are unique when applied to the character or nature of God Himself.

And so, the word, "magnify" as applied to God does not mean the same as it would when applied to things in the natural realm ...

YOU CANNOT MAKE GOD BIGGER

YOU CANNOT MAKE GOD GREATER

YOU CANNOT MAKE GOD MORE POWERFUL

YOU CANNOT CHANGE THE NATURE OR THE GLORY OF GOD

BUT YOU CAN CHANGE YOUR PERSPECTIVE OF HIM

It's a matter of **Perspective** ... noun

1.) a technique of depicting volumes and spatial relationships on a flat surface.

2.) a picture employing this technique, especially one in which it is prominent:

3.) a visible scene, especially one extending to a distance;

4.) the state of existing in space before the eye:

5.) the state of one's ideas, the facts known to one.

6.) the faculty of seeing all the relevant data in a meaningful relationship:

7.) a mental view or prospect:

Video – *Hubble Telescope's Biggest Discoveries – Part I*
(Feb. 24, 2017) CoconutScienceLab

"There are two trillion galaxies in the observable universe."

One of the ground breaking discoveries of the 20th century. **The accelerating expansion of the universe**. *(In other words, the universe is expanding or getting bigger!)*

Astronomers now believe that this expansion is driven by a mysterious **dark energy**.

Ex. 20:21 ... *"And the people stood afar off, and Moses drew near unto the thick darkness where God was."*

Deut. 4:11 ... *"And ye came near and stood under the mountain; and the mountain burned with fire unto the midst of heaven, with darkness, clouds, and thick darkness."*

Deut. 5:22 ... *"These words the LORD spake unto all your assembly in the mount out of the midst of the fire, of the cloud, and of the thick darkness, with a great voice: and he added no more. And he wrote them in two tables of stone, and delivered them unto me."*

II Chron. 6:1 ... *"Then spake Solomon, The LORD said that he would dwell in the thick darkness."*

Job 38:9 ... *"When I made the cloud the garment thereof, and thick darkness a swaddlingband for it,"*

THE HISTORY OF THE TELESCOPE

Before the telescope, men looked up into the black of night and saw stars, planets, etc. What they believed about the darkness of the night sky was determined by the perspective of unaided eyesight. But according to man's history, in 1609, a man in the Netherlands by the name of Hans Lippershey applied for a patent on a device called a telescope. Men would follow him and improve the device like Galileo who pointed it into the night sky. IT CHANGED THEIR PERSPECTIVE of the heavenlies.

Improvements were made in design, size and technology. And with each improvement it brought another CHANGE OF PERSPECTIVE. Till what we have today even after 20+ years is an orbiting telescope floating in the atmosphere of our planet, the Hubble space telescope.

PRAYER, PRAISE, AND WORSHIP ...

Does not make God bigger but it changes our PERSPECTIVE of a God who can only be understood and comprehended by changing our PERSPECTIVE OF HIM. The Psalmist wasn't trying to make God bigger, that's impossible, He already fills all in all. He already occupies everything we consider space and even perhaps expanding it.

What I want, what I believe God wants is to change our perspective through prayer and seeking Him.

Psalm 19:1 ... [[To the chief Musician, A Psalm of David.]] *The heavens declare the glory of God; and the firmament sheweth his handywork.*

(2) Day unto day uttereth speech, and night unto night sheweth knowledge.

(3) There is no speech nor language, where their voice is not heard.

(4) Their line is gone out through all the earth, and their words to the end of the world. In them hath he set a tabernacle for the sun,

(5) Which is as a bridegroom coming out of his chamber, and rejoiceth as a strong man to run a race.

(6) His going forth is from the end of the heaven, and his circuit unto the ends of it: and there is nothing hid from the heat thereof.

(7) The law of the LORD is perfect, converting the soul: the testimony of the LORD is sure, making wise the simple.

(8) The statutes of the LORD are right, rejoicing the heart: the commandment of the LORD is pure, enlightening the eyes.

(9) The fear of the LORD is clean, enduring for ever: the judgments of the LORD are true and righteous altogether.

(10) More to be desired are they than gold, yea, than much fine gold: sweeter also than honey and the honeycomb.

(11) Moreover by them is thy servant warned: and in keeping of them there is great reward.

(12) Who can understand his errors? cleanse thou me from secret faults.

(13) Keep back thy servant also from presumptuous sins; let them not have dominion over me: then shall I be upright, and I shall be innocent from the great transgression.

(14) Let the words of my mouth, and the meditation of my heart, be acceptable in thy sight, O LORD, my strength, and my redeemer."

PRAYER CHANGES OUR PERSPECTIVE OF HIM!

I will say it again. We will never make God any bigger than He already is. What we need to magnify is how we perceive Him. Your perspective of God is determined by how much of Him you want to see!

Chapter 10

Prayer & Preaching

Ezra 10:1 ... *"Now when Ezra had prayed, and when he had confessed, weeping and casting himself down before the house of God, there assembled unto him out of Israel a very great congregation of men and women and children: for the people wept very sore."*

Ezra 10:7-8 ... (7) *"And they made proclamation throughout Judah and Jerusalem unto all the children of the captivity, that they should gather themselves together unto Jerusalem;*

(8) And that whosoever would not come within three days, according to the counsel of the princes and the elders, all his substance should be forfeited, and himself separated from the congregation of those that had been carried away."

Neh. 8:1-8 ... (1) *"And all the people gathered themselves together as one man into the street that was before the water gate; and they spake unto Ezra the scribe to bring the book of the law of Moses, which the LORD had commanded to Israel.*

(2) And Ezra the priest brought the law before the congregation both of men and women, and all that could hear with understanding, upon the first day of the seventh month.

(3) And he read therein before the street that was before the water gate from the morning until midday, before the men and the

women, and those that could understand; and the ears of all the people were attentive unto the book of the law.

(4) And Ezra the scribe stood upon a pulpit of wood, which they had made for the purpose; and beside him stood Mattithiah, and Shema, and Anaiah, and Urijah, and Hilkiah, and Maaseiah, on his right hand; and on his left hand, Pedaiah, and Mishael, and Malchiah, and Hashum, and Hashbadana, Zechariah, and Meshullam.

(5) And Ezra opened the book in the sight of all the people; (for he was above all the people and when he opened it, all the people stood up:

(6) And Ezra blessed the LORD, the great God. And all the people answered, Amen, Amen, with lifting up their hands: and they bowed their heads, and worshipped the LORD with their faces to the ground.

*(7) Also Jeshua, and Bani, and Sherebiah, Jamin, Akkub, Shabbethai, Hodijah, Maaseiah, Kelita, Azariah, Jozabad, Hanan, Pelaiah, **and the Levites**, caused the people to understand the law: and the people stood in their place.*

(8) So they read in the book in the law of God distinctly, and gave the sense, and caused them to understand the reading."

LET'S CUT TO THE CHASE ...

In other words, let's get to the bottom line, the most important thing, ... when it comes to revival, which in my opinion means a powerful, effective, fruitful move of God. Souls saved, miracles displayed, lives transformed, and the Holy Ghost poured out. Yeah, I'm talking the Bible come to life before our eyes.

And it has been proven that it is very unlikely for that to happen unless prayer, fasting and preaching all come together in agreement. At this moment I would like to deal with two of those three. Prayer and Preaching. (Add fasting & you have a 3-fold cord)

They could be considered a double portion for God's people. Prayer is powerful and preaching is also powerful, but when you combine the two, they release the power of Almighty God upon the earth. So, if we are to have a great end-time harvest then we must have both prayer and preaching leading the way.

WHERE ARE THE PREACHERS?

There are eloquent speakers and then there are anointed preachers. A preacher isn't just the Pastor. According to the original Greek a preacher is someone who proclaims divine truth. So, I would say if you have believed and obeyed the scripture, and declare and share divine truth, YOU are a preacher ...

And Paul said this first ... Rom 10:14-15 ... (14) *"How then shall they call on him in whom they have not believed? And how shall they believe in him of whom they have not heard? And how shall they hear without a preacher?*

(15) And how shall they preach, except they be sent? As it is written, How beautiful are the feet of them that preach the gospel of peace, and bring glad tidings of good things!"

Not all preachers are Pastors but all Pastors are preachers. Same thing with the rest of the five-fold ministry. But if YOU are saved, then you are Called. If you are called you have the promise of the Holy Ghost, If you have the Holt Ghost you are Anointed. If you are anointed you have a Message. And if you have a message then you are a Preacher! BOOM!

Noah was called *a preacher of righteousness.* (II Pet. 2:5) He didn't have a church but he built an ark to the saving of his house. No, he didn't save the world but he saved his family! He never had a congregation of more than eight but that didn't stop him from preaching.

By the world's standard he wasn't successful. He never saw vast multitudes pray through, etc. But he had a message. A consistent, burning that he couldn't help but proclaim, even when it seemed like no one was listening.

And then we have Solomon, seven times in the book of Ecclesiastes he proclaims himself "the Preacher." He was probably everything we would expect from a "successful preacher." Money, reputation, wisdom, a large congregation, he had the temple, the singers, the musicians, power, influence, you name he had it. But what he didn't have when he wrote the book of Ecclesiastes was a relationship with God. In fact, Bible scholars believe that because of his many wives and their idols they robbed him of the anointing that he could have had in his later years.

So, there are preachers and then there are anointed preachers.

Leonard Ravenhill said this about "preachers" ...

When preachers lack unction, no one is fooled. That preacher has not gone far who, after he has ministered the Word, needs the back slap of friends or the stimulant of others' flattery in order to "feel good". The preacher who is elated over human praise for his preaching will sink under human criticism. This proves that he is walking in the flesh. A pastor can be inexpressibly happy after preaching a word from heaven even if his congregation storms at him.

WHAT WE NEED IS PRAYING PREACHERS ...

Yes, we need praying pastors, and praying apostles, and praying prophets, and praying evangelists, and praying teachers, but we need praying preachers! If you are a true believer, you are a preacher! And if you are a preacher you need to be a prayer warrior! Because without prayer your message won't be as effective.

There is prayer ... and then there is effectual fervent prayer. And if there is effectual, fervent prayer then there is also weak and ineffective prayer. And if your prayers are weak and ineffective your preaching will be weak and ineffective.

APOSTOLIC PRAYER CORPS.

When we were part of the congregation in Richmond, IN. I came up with what I thought was a cool idea for a prayer ministry. Literally make it like a military thing with military communication terms and such. With the Pastors approval, we assembled or tried to assemble what I perceived to be the most effective praying people in our assembly. The idea also included training and education on prayer just like the elite units of the military. Sharing various books on prayer. Having prayer summits & seminars with notable people sharing their experience and knowledge concerning prayer. (never got that far.)

But what I felt was the most important aspect of the Corps was that in every service there was someone in the Prayer Room praying for the Pastor as he preached the Word. Much like the ministry of Dwight L. Moody.

Dwight Moody saw thousands converted to Christ through his preaching. But what many don't know is that the secret of the success of his ministry were individuals who went down into the basement of the Church where Moody preached. They had no comfortable prayer room. No carpet, no padded chairs, nothing but a place to kneel and put their face between their knees and seek God for a mighty move of God on souls through Moody's preaching. And God answered.

WHAT WE NEED IN 2020 AND BEYOND IS ...

ANOINTED PREACHERS WHO PRAY ...

Acts 4:30-31 ... (30) *"By stretching forth thine hand to heal; and that signs and wonders may be done by the name of thy holy child Jesus.*

(31) **And when they had prayed***, the place was shaken where they were assembled together; and they were all filled with the Holy Ghost, and they spake the word of God with boldness."*

Chapter 11

"Prayer is _____"

Adapted from Week -

"Celebration of Prayer Series" – 09/03/2017

Lesson Text: Matthew 5:5-15

(5) And when thou prayest, thou shalt not be as the hypocrites are: for they love to pray standing in the synagogues and in the corners of the streets, that they may be seen of men. Verily I say unto you, They have their reward.

(6) But thou, when thou prayest, enter into thy closet, and when thou hast shut thy door, pray to thy Father which is in secret; and thy Father which seeth in secret shall reward thee openly.

(7) But when ye pray, use not vain repetitions, as the heathen do: for they think that they shall be heard for their much speaking.

(8) Be not ye therefore like unto them: for your Father knoweth what things ye have need of, before ye ask him.

(9) After this manner therefore pray ye: Our Father which art in heaven, Hallowed be thy name.

(10) Thy kingdom come. Thy will be done in earth, as it is in heaven.

(11) Give us this day our daily bread.

(12) And forgive us our debts, as we forgive our debtors.

(13) And lead us not into temptation, but deliver us from evil: For thine is the kingdom, and the power, and the glory, for ever. Amen.

(14) For if ye forgive men their trespasses, your heavenly Father will also forgive you:

(15) But if ye forgive not men their trespasses, neither will your Father forgive your trespasses."

PRAYER IS UNIVERSAL ...

In my deepest, darkest moments, what really got me through was a prayer. Sometimes my prayer was 'Help me.' Sometimes a prayer was 'Thank you.' What I've discovered is that intimate connection and communication with my creator will always get me through because I know my support, my help, is just a prayer away. —Ilyanla Vanzant

Prayer is not asking. It is the longing of the soul.
— Mahatma Gandi

Prayer is man's greatest power! – W. Clement Stone

Prayer is a strong wall and is a fortress of the church; it is a goodly Christian weapon. —Martin Luther

Prayer is an act of love. – Saint Theresa of Avila

True prayer is neither a mere mental exercise neither a vocal performance. It is far deeper than that- it is a spiritual transaction with the Creator of heaven and earth.

—Charles Spurgeon

Prayer is a confession of one's own worthiness and weakness.
—Mahatma Gandi

Prayer is the beginning and the end, the source and the fruit, the core and the content, the basis and goal of all peacemaking.

—Henri Nouwen

Prayer is our invitation to God to intervene in the affairs of earth. It is our request to work His ways in this world.

—Myles Munroe

Prayer doesn't change things- it changes us. If we are diligent in seeking God, slowly and surely we become better people.

—Joyce Meyer

Prayer is omnipotent: it's breath can melt the rocks- it's touch can break the stoutest chains. —William Lloyd Garrison

For me, prayer is not an opportunity to manipulate God, into doing what you want Him to do. Prayer is an opportunity to have a conversation with God to try to get in tune with His will.

—Francis Collins

Prayer is as a natural expression of faith as breathing is of life.

—Jonathan Edwards

> *Prayer is not an old woman's idle amusement. Properly understood and applied it is the most potent instrument of action.* —Mahatma Gandi
>
> *Prayer is where the action is.* —John Wesley

This is what I think we think prayer is ...

  ... 911

  ... a desperate request for a desperate need.

  ... the knot at the end of the rope.

  ... the last resort.

  ... an inconvenient obligation.

  ... a duty, a requirement.

  ... an opportunity to fall asleep.

  ... an act of faith hoping for an immediate, visible result.

  ... a source of great power and a source of much guilt.

So, prayer and how we pray reveals our true nature and attitude toward God.

In Matthew 6:5-15 Jesus teaches three things ...

1.) How not to pray ...

    Hypocrites and heathen ...

Matt. 6:5 ... *And when thou prayest, thou shalt not be* **as the hypocrites are**: *for they love to pray standing in the synagogues and in the corners of the streets, that they may be seen of men.*

    Hypocrite ... an actor, stage player, a pretender.

(Does that mean we shouldn't pray in public?)

Matt. 6:7 ... *"But when ye pray, use not vain repetitions, as the heathen do: for they think that they shall be heard for their much speaking."*

> *Heathen ... a Gentile* (vain repetitions)
> "Hail, Mary full of grace." (???)

(Can repeating the Lord's Prayer over and over be considered the same?)

(Why do we think we have to pray hours and hours and hours to be effective in prayer?)

2.) Where to pray ...

Matt. 6:6 ... *"But thou, when thou prayest, enter into thy closet, and when thou hast shut thy door, ..."*

The original Greek meaning of the word closet is ...*a storeroom, inner chamber, a secret, private place.*

Does that mean to literally shut ourselves in a closet? Maybe, maybe not, but the principle is to find a place with the least amount of distractions. Perhaps that's why Jesus always tried to found a quiet solitary place to pray. Yep, it's that important.

3.) How to pray the right way ...

Matt. 6:9 ... *"After this manner therefore pray ye: ..."*

NOT JUST SOMETHING TO BE TO BE QUOTED, but an example to be practiced, not just willy-nilly or whatever comes to mind, but with order and purpose.

There are six parts to a powerful, effective prayer. If we do them in His order than we are ushered into His presence and can accomplish more in prayer than we ever could praying our own way...

Prayer Is _____

A.) Praise the Name!

"Our Father which art in heaven, Hallowed be thy name."

B.) Pray for His Kingdom and His will to be done.

"Thy kingdom come. Thy will be done in earth, as it is in heaven."

C.) Pray for Your daily needs ... after praise and submission.

"Give us this day our daily bread."

D.) Pray for forgiveness ... for yourself and others. (Forgive yourself -guilt)

"And forgive us our debts, as we forgive our debtors."

E.) Pray for guidance and protection ...

"And lead us not into temptation, but deliver us from evil:"

F.) Thank Him! Praise Him! Give Him glory for the seen and the unseen. The done and the undone! The visible and the invisible!

"... for thine is the kingdom, and the power, and the glory, for ever. Amen."

WHY? BECAUSE ...

Without prayer we're lost...

Without proper prayer we won't have His presence ...

Without proper prayer we're weak and ineffective ...

Without proper prayer we're without the gifts and blessings of God ...

Without proper prayer we're without forgiveness and the ability to truly forgive ...

Without proper prayer we're directionless and without protection ...

Without proper prayer we don't possess His power and glory!

The Last Prayer of John Knox

While very ill, John Knox, the founder of the Presbyterian Church in Scotland, called to his wife and said, "Read me that Scripture where I first cast my anchor." After he listened to the beautiful prayer of Jesus recorded in John 17, he seemed to forget his weakness. He began to pray, interceding earnestly for his fellow men. He prayed for the ungodly who had rejected the gospel. He pleaded in behalf of people who had been recently converted. And he requested protection for the Lord's servants, many of whom were facing persecution. As Knox prayed, his spirit went home to be with the Lord. The man of whom Queen Mary had said, "I fear his prayers more than I do the armies of my enemies," ministered through prayer until the moment of his death. (Our Daily Bread. April 11).

Chapter 12

Praying in the Spirit

Rom. 8:26-27 KJV ... (26) *"Likewise the Spirit also helpeth our infirmities: for we know not what we should pray for as we ought: but the Spirit itself maketh intercession for us with groanings which cannot be uttered.*

(27) And he that searcheth the hearts knoweth what is the mind of the Spirit, because he maketh intercession for the saints according to the will of God."

SOME THINGS ARE SPOKEN BY COMMANDMENT & SOME THINGS BY PERMISSION

KEVIN ZADAI TESTIMONY

Kevin Zadai was a flight attendant for many years, but his hearts desire was to be in the ministry. He went into the dentist's office one day for some oral surgery and for some reason died during the procedure. His testimony is that when he died he went to heaven and talked with Jesus. His testimony is lengthy, but bottom line is that Jesus sent him back to earth to a large group of people. He not only came back with full recall of the incident, but has a prayer ministry including praying in the Spirit, and has been gifted with the ability to play several different instruments. He has recorded prayer music in which does the majority of the music himself. Here is a quote from Kevin Zadai's testimony ...

"Beyond anything else you could do on this earth the only thing He would want you to do is yield to the Spirit of God and that would bring forth an utterance called speaking in tongues and if you will pray in the Spirit and bring out the depths and the mysteries of God out into this realm that the spiritual realm would be so close to me that I would operate in the spiritual realm here on earth."

THIS IS NOT NECESSARILY ABOUT SPIRITUAL GIFTS ...

But the thing I've come to believe is that all the spiritual gifts are available to all believers if they want them. *"Covet earnestly the best gifts."* (I Cor. 12:31) The way I understand it, each believer is promised the Holy Ghost to empower them. (Acts 1:8) But the gifts of the Spirit are to help the natural man (who is already filled with the Holy Ghost) operate in the supernatural realm.

If you don't use the gifts available to you, then you are trying to accomplish the supernatural with carnal or natural ability. It doesn't work.

Enter the subject of Tongues. Number one, here again it's an experience designed for every believer. But there seems to be some confusion as to what speaking in tongues is all about. (I do know it's not of the devil.) The devil might try to duplicate it or replicate it but then discerning is required. (A whole different lesson)

So, in a nutshell I'll try to explain it as I know it. One of the first mentions of tongues is Isaiah 28:11-12 ...

(11) "For with stammering lips and another tongue will he speak to this people.

(12) To whom he said, This is the rest wherewith ye may cause the weary to rest; and this is the refreshing: yet they would not hear."

Then of course there's Acts 2 on the Day of Pentecost where the Holy Ghost was given to all those who were in the upper room.

This speaking in tongues in Acts 2 is a sign or evidence that they received it.

Acts 2:4 ... *"And they were all filled with the Holy Ghost, and began to speak with other tongues, as the Spirit gave them utterance."*

This is a sign of receiving the gift of the Holy Ghost.

Then Paul later instructs the Church in I Corinthians 14 about the gift of tongues, which isn't quite the same as in Acts 2. The gift of tongues and the interpretation of tongues is the supernatural ability to operate in an unknown language. It is a spiritual gift to a Holy Ghost filled believer who has already received the Acts 2 experience.

This is also a sign but it is a sign of the operation of God or the confirmation of the presence of God in the midst of His people.

But then in that same chapter Paul talks about tongues in connection to prayer. Some call it their prayer language.

HAVE YOU EVER STRUGGLED IN PRAYER?

It's funny I've got no problem vocalizing my own needs and wants. But when I begin to move into the deeper part of prayer, (some of us never get there all the time), I struggle with HOW to pray.

"... for we know not what we should pray for as we ought..." (Text vs. 26)

I believe Paul makes a fairly clear distinction in chapter 14. When in a public or semi-public atmosphere prayer should be in the common language for the sake of understanding. So, prayer in the setting described in I Corinthians 14 is for the group. But when it's just me and the Lord, praying in tongues is also for my edification, my strength, my direct communication with the understanding that I really don't know how to pray. The Spirit uses my human lips, my human tongue and my human voice to speak in an unknown language so that I can pray with greater power and authority releasing the power of God so that angels can be dispatched according to His will.

HERE'S OUR MISSION ...

To learn to yield our human will and emotions to the Spirit of God in prayer. Let Him speak through us so that we can accomplish His purpose, with His wisdom, and His ability.

Rom. 8:26 ... Amplified Bible *"So too the (Holy) Spirit comes to our aid and bears us up in our weakness; for we do not know what prayer to offer nor how to offer it worthily as we ought, but the Spirit Himself goes to meet our supplication and pleads in our behalf with unspeakable yearnings and groanings too deep for utterance."*

Chapter 13

The Power of Words

Part III

Psalm 5:1-3 ... *[[To the chief Musician upon Nehiloth (a pipe or flute plural), A Psalm of David.]] (1) "Give ear to my words, O LORD, consider my meditation.*

*(2) **Hearken unto the voice of my cry**, my King, and my God: for unto thee will I pray.*

*(3) **My voice shalt thou hear in the morning**, O LORD; in the morning will I direct my prayer unto thee, and will look up."*

Psalm 102:1 ... *"**Hear my prayer**, O LORD, and let my cry come unto thee."*

Psalm 19:14 ... *"**Let the words of my mouth**, and the meditation of my heart, be acceptable in thy sight, O LORD, my strength, and my redeemer."*

Psalm 54:2 ... *"Hear my prayer, O God; **give ear to the words of my mouth**."*

FOR CRYING OUT LOUD!

The human voice is one of the most powerful weapons ever created. The prayers spoken by a human voice activate powers far beyond our comprehension. Whether for good or for evil the principle remains the same.

A quick review of parts 1 & 2 reveals this about the power of the spoken word and the power of prayer spoken out loud.

Ecc. 8:4 ... *"Where the word of a king is, there is power: and who may say unto him, What doest thou?"* (Little "k" refers to an earthly king)

Prayer is the spoken expression of a human heart and mind. If prayer is words spoken into the atmosphere, your prayers spoken out loud have a powerful affect both on earth and in heaven.

Matt. 8:8 ... *"The centurion answered and said, Lord, I am not worthy that thou shouldest come under my roof: but speak the word only, and my servant shall be healed."*

The power of words is not in the thinking of them, or in the reading of them, or the writing of them, but in the speaking of them. EVERY human word spoken affects the environment, and every dimension.

My prayers do not have to necessarily be spontaneous in origin, but they do have to be audible. The sound of my voice is what heaven and hell will hear, it is my voice which looses or binds things, it's my voice that releases my faith in God's power, it's my voice that sets the enemy to flight and releases the will of God not my thoughts!

The Prayer of Elijah ...

(36) And it came to pass at the time of the offering of the evening sacrifice, that Elijah the prophet came near, and said, LORD God of Abraham, Isaac, and of Israel, let it be known this day that thou art God in Israel, and that I am thy servant, and that I have done all these things at thy word.

(37) Hear me, O LORD, hear me, that this people may know that thou art the LORD God, and that thou hast turned their heart back again. (63 words brought down fire from heaven)

Also, the prayer, the words spoken or prophesied by Ezekiel released the power to transform a valley of dead dry bones into a living, breathing, exceeding great army.

We also need to put into practice speaking the Word of God and also praying the Word of God out loud. If the Word of God is swift and powerful as a two-edged sword when we read it, why wouldn't it be as much or even more powerful when we pray it? Don't just read the Word of God, speak the Word of God out loud, pray the Word of God out loud!

IF THERE IS EFFECTUAL PRAYER & THERE IS ALSO INEFFECTUAL PRAYER ...

James 5:16b ... *"The effectual fervent prayer of a righteous man availeth much."*

In the English translation of the word "effectual" it is an adjective (although in the KJV Greek it's a verb) and has these two meanings ...

1.) producing or capable of producing an intended effect; adequate.

2.) valid or binding, as an agreement or document.

It also gives these related words ... *effective, capable, conclusive, decisive, efficient, forcible, lawful, legal, potent, powerful, productive, sound, strong.*

My point is this, if prayer can be effectual, then logic dictates that prayer may also be "ineffectual" or just the opposite as in ...

... ineffective, incapable, inconclusive, indecisive, inefficient, unlawful, illegal, impotent, powerless, unproductive, & weak.

THE MOST INEFECTUAL PRAYER,
EVEN OF A RIGHTEOUS MAN ...

Is the prayer that is never spoken out loud. It may even have an element of faith, but without becoming spoken words, it could hinder God's answer. Now I will qualify that statement that God does know our heart & mind (unlike the enemy) and so He does have the ability to perform our requests by knowing the desires of your heart, even if it's not vocalized properly.

I have pointed out in previous lessons that God may have the ability to know your thoughts and He may already have an answer prepared but He may be waiting for you to SPEAK THE WORDS, not just think the thought.

Matt. 6:8 ... *"Be not ye therefore like unto them: for your Father knoweth what things ye have need of, **before ye ask him**."*

Just because God already knows what you need, doesn't mean that you don't necessarily have to ask. And if He requires you to ask than the only truly effective way that an answer can be accomplished is through your audible human speech.

THE CHURCH HAS BECOME ...
"THE SILENCE OF THE LAMBS"

Something is wrong with the Church. It's not the same Church in the book of Acts. The building doesn't shake when we pray. Why not? The Holy Ghost is the same. The power of God hasn't changed. God is still no respecter of persons. So, what's the problem?

Lack of faith? Lack of commitment? Lack of consecration? Maybe all the above. But I believe it's because the Church has become "dumb." We have allowed the enemy to steal our voice in prayer!

Isaiah 10:5-14 ... (5) *"O Assyrian, the rod of mine anger, and the staff in their hand is mine indignation.*

(6) I will send him (Assyria) against an hypocritical nation, and against the people of my wrath (That's His own people) will I give him a charge, to take the spoil, and to take the prey, and to tread them down like the mire of the streets.

(7) Howbeit he (Assyria) meaneth not so, neither doth his heart think so; but it is in his heart to destroy and cut off nations not a few.

(8) For he saith, Are not my princes altogether kings?

(9) Is not Calno as Carchemish? is not Hamath as Arpad? is not Samaria as Damascus?

(10) As my hand hath found the kingdoms of the idols, and whose graven images did excel them of Jerusalem and of Samaria;

(11) Shall I not, as I have done unto Samaria and her idols, so do to Jerusalem and her idols?

(12) Wherefore it shall come to pass, that when the Lord hath performed his whole work upon mount Zion and on Jerusalem, I will punish the fruit of the stout heart of the king of Assyria, and the glory of his high looks.

(13) For he saith, By the strength of my hand I (Assyria) have done it, and by my wisdom; for I am prudent: and I have removed

the bounds of the people, and have robbed their treasures, and I have put down the inhabitants like a valiant man: (But in reality God allowed it ...)

(14) And my hand hath found as a nest the riches of the people: and as one gathereth eggs that are left, have I gathered all the earth; <u>and there was none that moved the wing, or opened the mouth, or peeped.</u>"

The enemy is most effective when they come in by infiltration and stealth. If God's people are preoccupied, distracted and silent, then the enemy can steal everything!

You want to know when we get excited and begin to pray like there's no tomorrow? When there's rioting in the streets! When there's fires burning! When there's looting and destruction! When they're making us stay inside and wear masks! And THEN we all stand there and ask ourselves how did this happen?!?! Well, I believe I have an answer. WE HAVE BEEN CAPTURED AND MUZZLED ...

Are You Familiar With the Spiked Gag Mask That Slave Women Were Required to Wear for an ENTIRE GENERATION Until Our Native Tongue Was Forgotten? It Not Only Covered the Mouth But Had Blades in the Mouth to Cut With Even the Slightest Movement of the Tongue. Do You Know Why?

According to Several Captains Logs, the Women Were Said to Have the Power to Speak Enchantments That Would Cause Slave Takers to Drop Dead on the Spot. So They Silenced Them and Took Away the Language and Deminized All Indigenous Forms of Worship and Ritual.

#KNOWThyself
#NJKwame

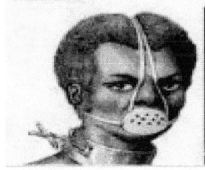
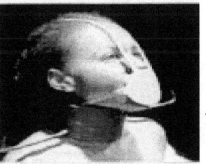

www.onsizzle.com

Please also note that their eyes were not covered so they were able to see; their ears weren't stopped, so they could hear; their noses weren't covered so they could smell; they still could think, perceive, and function on a high level; they were alive & they could breathe, they could eat but perhaps very little to keep them weak; but other than the mask / gag they would have been able to do practically everything but SPEAK!

WHEN THE CHURCH FAILS TO PRAY ... WE ARE DUMB!

Do you really think God would allow all this evil if the Church was exercising true prayer? It's not God fault! It's not the Devil's fault! It's not Trump's fault or even Obama, Hillary or Biden! You want to know whose fault it is???? It's the Church's fault!!! We have allowed the enemy to not only lull us into submission, but we have allowed him to steal our prosperity and promises. We have been captured and conquered without a fight! And we have allowed him to steal the power of our prayers! A silent Church is a Church without prayer, promises or power. Victory depends on our voice! Upon our ability to speak the words of life! To pray the effectual fervent prayers of faith! To speak the pure Word of God into this world for salvation, deliverance, and healing.

WE NEED TO FIND OUR VOICE ...

Psalm 38:13 ... *"But I, as a deaf man, heard not; and I was as a dumb man that openeth not his mouth."*

Psalm 39:2 ... *"I was dumb with silence, I held my peace, even from good; and my sorrow was stirred."*

Psalm 39:9 ... *"I was dumb, I opened not my mouth; because thou didst it."*

Proverbs 31:8 ... "<u>Open thy mouth for the dumb</u> in the cause of all such as are appointed to destruction."

Isaiah 35:6 ... "Then shall the lame man leap as an hart, <u>and the tongue of the dumb sing</u>: for in the wilderness shall waters break out, and streams in the desert."

Isaiah 56:10 ... "His watchmen are blind: they are all ignorant, <u>they are all dumb dogs, they cannot bark</u>; sleeping, lying down, loving to slumber."

Ezekiel 24:27 ... "In that day shall thy mouth be opened to him which is escaped, and thou shalt speak, <u>and be no more dumb</u>: and thou shalt be a sign unto them; and they shall know that I am the LORD."

Ezekiel 33:22 ... "Now the hand of the LORD was upon me in the evening, afore he that was escaped came; and had opened my mouth, until he came to me in the morning; and my mouth was opened, and <u>I was no more dumb</u>."

Hmmmmmmmm. It's kind of funny that in Ezekiel 3:26 God told Ezekiel that he would be "dumb." But after chapter 33 he had regained his speech. God told him to prophesy to the bones and to the wind then in chapter 37. Would that exceeding great army ever have been raised up if Ezekiel was "dumb"?

HELEN KELLER, WHO IS SHE?

At 19 months of age Helen Keller contracted an illness that caused not only blindness, but deafness as well. Because she couldn't hear it also rendered her ability to speak useless. She was for all intents and purposes totally unable to express herself through speech until the age of 7 when her teacher Anne Sullivan finally devised a method to communicate with Helen and in turn, she regained her ability to speak.

This author says this of Helen Keller ... Vicky Newman, Evangelical, charismatic Christian

"Having vocal chords intact and working, Helen could speak. She just didn't know a thing such as speech existed. She could not understand or control anything in her world. She saw only darkness. She heard only silence. What could such a person possibly contribute to the greater world? In fact, her contributions are still in play, teaching the world not to sell short someone with disabilities."

And in Helen's own words she expresses the miracle that led to the restoration of her ability to speak ...

Writing in her autobiography, The Story of My Life, Keller recalled the moment: "I stood still, my whole attention fixed upon the motions of her fingers. Suddenly I felt a misty consciousness as of something forgotten — a thrill of returning thought; and somehow the mystery of language was revealed to me. I knew then that w-a-t-e-r meant the wonderful cool something that was flowing over my hand. The living word awakened my soul, gave it light, hope, set it free!"[13] (From Wikipedia)

Chapter 14

"So What!"

Isaiah 1:1-20

(1) The vision of Isaiah the son of Amoz, which he saw concerning Judah and Jerusalem in the days of Uzziah, Jotham, Ahaz, and Hezekiah, kings of Judah.

(2) Hear, O heavens, and give ear, O earth: for the LORD hath spoken, I have nourished and brought up children, and they have rebelled against me.

(3) The ox knoweth his owner, and the ass his master's crib: but Israel doth not know, my people doth not consider.

(4) Ah sinful nation, a people laden with iniquity, a seed of evildoers, children that are corrupters: they have forsaken the LORD, they have provoked the Holy One of Israel unto anger, they are gone away backward.

(5) Why should ye be stricken any more? ye will revolt more and more: the whole head is sick, and the whole heart faint.

(6) From the sole of the foot even unto the head there is no soundness in it; but wounds, and bruises, and putrifying sores: they have not been closed, neither bound up, neither mollified with ointment.

(7) Your country is desolate, your cities are burned with fire: your land, strangers devour it in your presence, and it is desolate, as overthrown by strangers.

(8) And the daughter of Zion is left as a cottage in a vineyard, as a lodge in a garden of cucumbers, as a besieged city.

(9) Except the LORD of hosts had left unto us a very small remnant, we should have been as Sodom, and we should have been like unto Gomorrah.

(10) Hear the word of the LORD, ye rulers of Sodom; give ear unto the law of our God, ye people of Gomorrah.

*(11) **To what purpose is the multitude of your sacrifices unto me? saith the LORD: I am full of the burnt offerings of rams, and the fat of fed beasts; and I delight not in the blood of bullocks, or of lambs, or of he goats.***

(12) When ye come to appear before me, who hath required this at your hand, to tread my courts?

(13) Bring no more vain oblations; incense is an abomination unto me; the new moons and sabbaths, the calling of assemblies, I cannot away with; it is iniquity, even the solemn meeting.

(14) Your new moons and your appointed feasts my soul hateth: they are a trouble unto me; I am weary to bear them.

(15) And when ye spread forth your hands, I will hide mine eyes from you: yea, when ye make many prayers, I will not hear: your hands are full of blood.

(16) Wash you, make you clean; put away the evil of your doings from before mine eyes; cease to do evil;

(17) Learn to do well; seek judgment, relieve the oppressed, judge the fatherless, plead for the widow.

(18) Come now, and let us reason together, saith the LORD: though your sins be as scarlet, they shall be as white as snow; though they be red like crimson, they shall be as wool.

(19) If ye be willing and obedient, ye shall eat the good of the land:

(20) But if ye refuse and rebel, ye shall be devoured with the sword: for the mouth of the LORD hath spoken it."

WE HUMANS OVERTHINK EVERYTHING...

Have you noticed that we live in a day where everything is to the extreme? There used to be, although it's hard to remember, a middle ground on a lot of issues. But now you're either right wing or left wing. You're either black or white. You're either a 1%er or a 99%er. (You know, either very rich or very dependent on the government.) You're either up or you're down. You're either pro or against. You're either original recipe or extra crispy!

We have become a generation of overthinkers and under-achievers. The problem is that God's people allow that kind of thinking in the church. Now before we overthink this, let's set some parameters. Let's take one thing and clarify this thought. As difficult as that might be, (because we all know everything that's wrong with the church, right? Somebody should write a book!), let's talk about ...

SACRIFICES!

Oh yeah, don't get me started on sacrifices. If we had the time and energy, we could talk about all the sacrifices we've made for God. All the money we give, the movie and game time we give up to come to church, the Saturdays AND Sundays we give to God. Blah, blah, blah, blah. In fact, I sacrifice so much, I sacrifice my sacrifices to sacrifice.

The word sacrifice is both a noun & a verb... As a noun it means ...

1.) *the offering of animal, plant, or human life or of some material possession to a deity, as in propitiation or homage.*

2.) *the person, animal, or thing so offered.*

3.) *the surrender or destruction of something prized or desirable for the sake of something considered as having a higher or more pressing claim.*

4.). *the thing so surrendered or devoted.*

> *5.) a loss incurred in selling something below its value.*

As a verb it carries these definitions ...

> *7.) to make a sacrifice or offering of.*

> *8.) to surrender or give up, or permit injury or disadvantage to, for the sake of something else.*

> *9.) to dispose of (goods, property, etc.) regardless of profit.*

Based on those definitions, I guess the question shouldn't be, "What have you sacrificed?" But maybe it should be, "Why, are you making those sacrifices?"

LET'S LET THAT ONE SIMMER ON THE BACK BURNER ...

"Let's look at some scripture ...

1 Chron. 29:20-21 ... (20) *And David said to all the congregation, Now bless the LORD your God. And all the congregation blessed the LORD God of their fathers, and bowed down their heads, and worshipped the LORD, and the king.*

*(21) And they sacrificed sacrifices unto the LORD, and offered burnt offerings unto the LORD, on the morrow after that day, **even a thousand bullocks, a thousand rams, and a thousand lambs, with their drink offerings, and sacrifices in abundance for all Israel**:"*

2 Chron. 7:4-7 ... (4) *"Then the king and all the people offered sacrifices before the LORD.*

*(5) And king Solomon offered **a sacrifice of twenty and two thousand oxen, and an hundred and twenty thousand sheep**: so the king and all the people dedicated the house of God.*
(Who decided how many of each?)

(6) And the priests waited on their offices: the Levites also with

instruments of musick of the LORD, which David the king had made to praise the LORD, because his mercy endureth for ever, when David praised by their ministry; and the priests sounded trumpets before them, and all Israel stood.

(7) Moreover Solomon hallowed the middle of the court that was before the house of the LORD: for there he offered burnt offerings, and the fat of the peace offerings, because the brasen altar which Solomon had made was not able to receive the burnt offerings, and the meat offerings, and the fat."

I Kings 8:5 ... "And king Solomon, and all the congregation of Israel, that were assembled unto him, were with him before the ark, **sacrificing sheep and oxen, that could not be told nor numbered for multitude**."

WHAT VALUE DID GOD PUT ON ALL THOSE SACRIFICES?
DID THEY MOVE GOD? OR DID GOD SHRUG & SAY "SO WHAT"

THE PURPOSE OF THE LAW WAS NOT TO SATISFY THE NEED FOR BLOOD,
BUT TO POINT US TO CHRIST!

Heb. 10:1 ... "For the law having a shadow of good things to come, and not the very image of the things, can never with those sacrifices which they offered year by year continually make the comers thereunto perfect."

Heb. 10:3 ... "But in those sacrifices there is a remembrance again made of sins every year."

"So What!"

Heb. 10:6 ... *"In burnt offerings and sacrifices for sin thou hast had no pleasure."*

Heb. 10:11 ... *"And every priest standeth daily ministering and offering oftentimes the same sacrifices, which can never take away sins:"*

Heb. 13:16 ... *"But to do good and to communicate forget not: for with such sacrifices God is well pleased."*

1 Peter 2:5 ... *"Ye also, as lively stones, are built up a spiritual house, an holy priesthood, to offer up spiritual sacrifices, acceptable to God by Jesus Christ."*

GOD DOESN'T WANT OR NEED MORE SACRIFICES ...

He just wants you to give what is required with a proper attitude and spirit!

Psalm 51:17 ... *"The sacrifices of God are a broken spirit: a broken and a contrite heart, O God, thou wilt not despise."*

When you think that you've sacrificed enough, ask yourself how much Jesus sacrificed!

GOD SAYS, "YOU DON'T IMPRESS ME MUCH WITH ALL YOUR SACRIFICES" ...

Yes, prayer is a sacrifice, fasting is a sacrifice, going to church is a sacrifice, living holy and godly in this present world is a sacrifice, giving tithes and offerings is a sacrifice, being honest is a sacrifice, loving sinners and some saints is a sacrifice ... And there are times when God says, I love you but "So What!"

WHY are you doing what you're doing is just as important to God as to WHAT you are doing!

Chapter 15

Stay Empty

Ruth 1:1-22

(1) "Now it came to pass in the days when the judges ruled, that there was a famine in the land. And a certain man of Bethlehemjudah went to sojourn in the country of Moab, he, and his wife, and his two sons.

(2) And the name of the man was Elimelech, and the name of his wife Naomi, and the name of his two sons Mahlon and Chilion, Ephrathites of Bethlehemjudah. And they came into the country of Moab, and continued there.

(3) And Elimelech Naomi's husband died; and she was left, and her two sons.

(4) And they took them wives of the women of Moab; the name of the one was Orpah, and the name of the other Ruth: and they dwelled there about ten years.

(5) And Mahlon and Chilion died also both of them; and the woman was left of her two sons and her husband.

(6) Then she arose with her daughters in law, that she might return from the country of Moab: for she had heard in the country of Moab how that the LORD had visited his people in giving them bread.

(7) Wherefore she went forth out of the place where she was, and her two daughters in law with her; and they went on the way to return unto the land of Judah.

(8) And Naomi said unto her two daughters in law, Go, return

each to her mother's house: the LORD deal kindly with you, as ye have dealt with the dead, and with me.

(9) The LORD grant you that ye may find rest, each of you in the house of her husband. Then she kissed them; and they lifted up their voice, and wept.

(10) And they said unto her, Surely we will return with thee unto thy people.

(11) And Naomi said, Turn again, my daughters: why will ye go with me? are there yet any more sons in my womb, that they may be your husbands?

(12) Turn again, my daughters, go your way; for I am too old to have an husband. If I should say, I have hope, if I should have an husband also to night, and should also bear sons;

(13) Would ye tarry for them till they were grown? would ye stay for them from having husbands? nay, my daughters; for it grieveth me much for your sakes that the hand of the LORD is gone out against me.

(14) And they lifted up their voice, and wept again: and Orpah kissed her mother in law; but Ruth clave unto her.

(15) And she said, Behold, thy sister in law is gone back unto her people, and unto her gods: return thou after thy sister in law.

(16) And Ruth said, Intreat me not to leave thee, or to return from following after thee: for whither thou goest, I will go; and where thou lodgest, I will lodge: thy people shall be my people, and thy God my God:

(17) Where thou diest, will I die, and there will I be buried: the LORD do so to me, and more also, if ought but death part thee and me.

(18) When she saw that she was stedfastly minded to go with her, then she left speaking unto her.

(19) So they two went until they came to Bethlehem. And it came

to pass, when they were come to Bethlehem, that all the city was moved about them, and they said, Is this Naomi?

(20) And she said unto them, Call me not Naomi, call me Mara: for the Almighty hath dealt very bitterly with me.

*(21) **I went out full, and the LORD hath brought me home again empty**: why then call ye me Naomi, seeing the LORD hath testified against me, and the Almighty hath afflicted me?*

(22) So Naomi returned, and Ruth the Moabitess, her daughter in law, with her, which returned out of the country of Moab: and they came to Bethlehem in the beginning of barley harvest."

THE MOST INTERESTING MAN IN THE WORLD...
"STAY THIRSTY, MY FRIENDS!"

We believe in being full. In fact, if we're not full, we think that is the only way we ought to be. Don't get me wrong there's nothing wrong with being full of the Holy Ghost, full of grace and truth, full of the righteousness, full of peace, full of joy, full of whatever. We are hard wired to want to be "full."

Our misconception of "full" is that we should always be full. But in reality, you can never be full unless sometimes you are empty (Or less than full). Does that make sense?

But think about it ...

If we are always full of God then that also means we are satisfied with what we are and what we've got right now. But God always has more than what you are filled with, so sometimes He allows us to get empty so He can fill us with more of Him!

God will always be bigger than the vessel He fills!

Gen. 31:42 ... This is Jacob on the way home from Laban's with two wives, 12 sons, and a bunch of livestock... You might say he was full ... But this is how he described himself ...

"Unless the God of my father, the God of Abraham and the Fear of Isaac, had been with me, surely now you would have sent me away empty-handed. God has seen my affliction and the labor of my hands, and rebuked you last night."

Twenty years earlier Jacob showed up at Laban's house empty. All he had was basically the clothes on his back, a sore neck from a rock pillow, a dream, and a promise from God. No blessing, no birthright, no money, no camels, no sheep, no cattle and no luck.

But as of verse 42 he had ... Two wives, two handmaidens, 12 sons, a daughter, a bunch of livestock, and a promise. If he had never experienced being empty, he would have never experienced what it was what like to be full.

---

2 Kings 4:3 ... The prophet speaks to the widow ... Before she could receive her miracle she had to be empty ... Before she could be full, she had to be empty.

"Then he said, Go, borrow thee vessels abroad of all thy neighbours, even empty vessels; borrow not a few."

Solomon said this about clouds that are full ...

Ecc. 11:3 ... *"If the clouds be full of rain, they empty themselves upon the earth: and if the tree fall toward the south, or toward the north, in the place where the tree falleth, there it shall be."*

Clouds are designed to empty out when they become full. They don't stay full and try to hold onto that rain. They release it and become empty again.

Isa. 29:8 ... *"It shall even be as when an hungry man dreameth, and, behold, he eateth; but he awaketh, and his soul is empty: or as when a thirsty man dreameth, and, behold, he drinketh; but he awaketh, and, behold, he is faint, and his soul hath appetite: so shall the multitude of all the nations be, that fight against mount Zion."*

Here's important thing to remember ... in the natural a hungry man will always seek food, a thirsty man will always crave liquid, a poor man will always seek riches but there comes a time that we also have the unnatural desire to stay full, stay satisfied, stay rich. But to the spiritual man we should never be full, never be satisfied, never think we have all of God we can obtain.

Luke 5:4-8 ... *"Now when he had left speaking, he said unto Simon, Launch out into the deep, and let down your nets for a draught.*

(5) And Simon answering said unto him, Master, we have toiled all the night, and have taken nothing: nevertheless at thy word I will let down the net.

(6) And when they had this done, they inclosed a great multitude of fishes: and their net brake.

(7) And they beckoned unto their partners, which were in the other ship, that they should come and help them. And they came, and filled both the ships, so that they began to sink.

(8) When Simon Peter saw it, he fell down at Jesus' knees, saying, Depart from me; for I am a sinful man, O Lord."

Full is good. Full is great. Full can be satisfying. But in order to be filled we've got to be empty!

The story of the song ...

"Fill My Cup, Lord"

Life was never to be a bed of roses for Richard Blanchard.

A severe lung problem developed, and Blanchard was left with one-third of his lung capacity. But a diminished physical well-being did not stop young Blanchard.

In 1953, he became the pastor of a church in Coral Gables, Florida, and one day, was asked by a young couple to perform their marriage ceremony. However, the couple was quite late for their counseling appointment.

Blanchard told his secretary, I will wait for thirty minutes and I'm leaving. He then went to a nearby Sunday school room and sat down to play the piano for a while.

He later said, When I was not in the mood to be used of God, God was in a mood to use me. In less than thirty-minutes, as he waited for the young couple, God gave him the inspiring song Fill My Cup, Lord.

As Richard Blanchard looks back over his life, he declares even though God chose in his providence to impair my physical being, he has in so many other ways 'Fill'd My Cup.'

Chapter 16

Strange Fire

Lev. 10:1-3 ... *"And Nadab and Abihu, the sons of Aaron, took either of them his censer, and put fire therein, and put incense thereon, and offered strange fire before the LORD, which he commanded them not.*

(2) And there went out fire from the LORD, and devoured them, and they died before the LORD.

(3) Then Moses said unto Aaron, This is it that the LORD spake, saying, I will be sanctified in them that come nigh me, and before all the people I will be glorified. And Aaron held his peace."

Num. 3:4 ... *"And Nadab and Abihu died before the LORD, when they offered strange fire before the LORD, in the wilderness of Sinai, and they had no children: and Eleazar and Ithamar ministered in the priest's office in the sight of Aaron their father."*

Num. 26:61 ... *"And Nadab and Abihu died, when they offered strange fire before the LORD."*

WHEN IT COMES TO UNDERSTSANDING THE O.T. ...

1 Cor. 10:11 ... "Now all these things happened unto them for

ensamples: and they are written for our admonition, upon whom the ends of the world are come."

If you read the previous ten verses you will find that Paul is talking about the Children of Israel after being brought out of Egypt under the leadership and the Law of Moses. The things which they experienced were real. But their experiences and the consequences of their actions are also meant to be types and shadow of what would come in the N.T. They were "physical" examples illustrating "spiritual" truths or principles for us today under the N.T. covenant and the kingdom of God.

NADAB & ABIHU ... NOT A RANDOM ACT DISOBEDIENCE

Again, if you read the preceding 2-3 chapters of our text, you find that these two men didn't just happen to wander into the Tabernacle and accidently offend God to the point where He used holy fire to incinerate them. They had been instructed directly from Moses and Aaron as to their duties and in what manner they were to be performed.

But a casual reading of those passages of scripture kind of produces the reaction,

Well, that's a pretty over the top and harsh way of dealing with what at first glance appears to be something relatively minor.

I mean this is the same God of love who declares that His mercy endures forever! (45 times that phrase is repeated in scripture.) I mean did they just happen to catch Him on a bad day?

Here is my opinion. God is both a God of love AND a God of judgment. Paul gives this explanation in ...

Rom 11:22 ... *"Behold therefore the goodness and severity of God: on them which fell, severity; but toward thee, goodness, if thou continue in his goodness: otherwise thou also shalt be cut off."*

Beginning at that line of thought, I can safely say these things about God ...

He knows the selfishness and wickedness of humanity. He knows that to be carnal is enmity towards Him. He also knows that we need salvation and restoration. So, He Himself has made a way so that we can be acceptable. It's called obedience and application of His word which includes repentance.

Think about the times, primarily in the O.T., where God pours out swift and severe judgement.

- Uzzah and the Ox cart.
- The guy who picked up sticks on the Sabbath (got stoned)
- David took a census ... God sent a plague & killed 70,000 men.
- Ananias & Sapphira

THE BOTTOM LINE IS GOD KNOWS ...

Jeremiah 17:9 ... "*The heart is deceitful above all things, and desperately wicked: who can know it?*"

Now getting back to Nadab and Abihu. By all outward appearances they didn't do anything worthy of a fiery death. I mean they seemed to be right in almost every way ...

They were called by name ... Aaron's son's

They had the proper garments ... (white linen garments)

They had been anointed with oil ...

They had made the proper sacrifices ...

They had applied the blood properly ... right ear, right thumb, & right big toe

They had the right incense ... incense is a type and shadow of prayer and praise.

But they were judged because of "strange fire."

Their "censers" represented their personal offering of prayer and praise to God. It wasn't what they offered in the way of "incense" that offended God, but where they got the fire. Or where they obviously didn't get it.

If you study closely, each time the priests offered incense on the altar of incense before the veil in the tabernacle there were two requirements, one that it had to be a specific blend of incense, and two it had to be lit or ignited by a coal from the brazen altar of sacrifice in the courtyard.

The sacrifice was always required before they could enter into the holy place. The blood always had to be shed and applied. And the same fire that consumed the sacrifice had to be mingled with the incense that was offered up to God for a sweet-smelling savour.

THE N.T. PRINCIPLE OR TYPE & SHADOW ...

In practically everything else they were acceptable to God. They had the right genealogy, the right dress, the right sacrifice, they were anointed, they had the right application of the blood, they had the right equipment, they even had the right incense, but they didn't have the right "fire."

The brazen altar represents N.T. repentance. It is the place where we leave not only our sins, but our attitudes and carnal desires. It's a place of death, but it is also the place where we get the fire for our prayer and praise. Without the fire from the place of death our prayers and praise are ignited by our own fleshly desires. Without the smell of death mingled with our petitions and praise we are offering God a sacrifice ignited with strange fire.

So here is the spiritual principle that must always accompany any prayer or praise of the N.T. church. If we are kings and priests unto God we can be properly dressed, we can do everything the right way, we can be anointed, and have the blood applied, and even be washed by the water of the Word, but if we offer up personal prayer and praise to God without repentance, then we are offering up personal prayer and praise with which may be considered by God as "strange fire."

WHAT DOES THAT MEAN?

It means that every time we go to God in prayer our hearts must be cleansed by repentance. It's as if you are trying to enter the Holy place with a heart that is wicked and therefore extremely offensive to God. The work of the Altar of Incense cannot be accepted without the work of the Brazen Altar of sacrifice. Worship and praise without repentance is filled with human vanity and pride. Therefore, God sees that as an attempt to steal His glory. And He will never allow that!

The prayer of daily repentance is the coal of fire that ignites and gives our prayers power and acceptability with God.

Chapter 17

The Power of Words

Part IV

"The human voice is one of the most powerful weapons ever created. The prayers spoken by a human voice activate powers far beyond our comprehension. Whether for good or for evil the principle remains the same." (Part III)

"Prayer is the spoken expression of a human heart and mind. If prayer are words spoken into the atmosphere, your prayers spoken out loud have a powerful affect both on earth and in heaven." (Part III)

"The power of words is not in the thinking of them, or in the reading of them, or the writing of them, but in the speaking of them. EVERY human word spoken affects the environment, and every dimension." (Part III)

"My prayers do not have to necessarily be spontaneous in origin, but they do have to be audible. The sound of my voice is what heaven and hell will hear, it is my voice which looses or binds things, it's my voice that releases my faith in God's power, it's my voice that sets the enemy to flight and releases the will of God not my thoughts!"(Part III)

"We also need to put into practice speaking the Word of God and also praying the Word of God out loud. If the Word of God is swift and powerful as a two-edged sword when we read it, why wouldn't it be as much or even more powerful when we pray it? Don't just read the Word of God, speak the Word of God out loud, pray the Word of God out loud!" (III)

THE MOST INEFECTUAL PRAYER, EVEN OF A RIGHTEOUS MAN ... *Is the prayer that is never spoken out loud. It may even have an element of faith, but without the spoken words it's impossible for God to answer it."*

"Do you really think God would allow all this evil if the Church was exercising true prayer? You want to know whose fault it is???? It's the Church's fault!!! We have allowed the enemy to not only lull us into submission, but we have allowed him to steal our prosperity and promises. We have been captured and conquered without a fight! And we have allowed him to steal our voice in the power of our prayers! A silent Church is a Church without prayer, promises or power. Victory depends on our voice! Victory depends upon our ability to speak the words of life! To pray out loud the effectual fervent prayers of faith! To speak the pure Word of God into this world for salvation, deliverance, and healing." (III)

"And so, if words have power, then prayers that are spoken have power. The difference between mere words spoken and prayer is that prayers are words spoken with faith." (Part II)

"If the human words spoken by Elijah had the power to call fire down fire from heaven, then how much more powerful would it be if we prayed the Word of God out loud?" (Part II)

From an internet article *"Praying God's Word Out Loud for a Spiritual Breakthrough"*

By Debbie Przybylski

In a similar way we have a powerful weapon—the Word of God. We can kick the enemy and defeat him by speaking the Word of God. Praying the Bible out loud is powerful for spiritual breakthrough. Praying God's Word with our lips is a dangerous weapon to Satan. He knows the power of the Word of God.

Many Christians do not realize that praying the Word out loud breaks through the enemy's defenses. It can bring destruction to his plans and bring victory to God's purposes. Let's not be ignorant of the power we have in the Bible. Let's learn to use the Word of God and speak it out loud for spiritual breakthrough. When we do, the spiritual atmosphere of entire cities can change. We can make a huge impact in our neighborhoods through praying or singing God's Word out loud and over it. The government of God is released through our prayers. (Part II)

"If we are human, then we all have been given a very powerful weapon. Words are one of the most powerful things God created. It was by His Words that He created everything and if we are created in His image than we have been endowed with at least the type and shadow of that power."

LET'S BEGIN IN I CORINTHIANS 14 ...

Paul's instruction on the use of tongues to the Church. It isn't instruction about the use of tongues to sinners. The people Paul is addressing have been filled with the Holy Ghost as part of the

New Birth experience Jesus taught in John 3 and Peter preached in Acts 2:38.

It is by no means to discourage the use of tongues in the Church or out of the Church. But is meant to encourage the proper use of tongues. Just so there is no mistake or misunderstanding ...

Tongues as defined by Nelson's Illus. Bible Dict. (Pg. 1060) is ... " *the Spirit-given ability to speak in a languages not known to the speaker or in an ecstatic language that could not normally be understood by the speaker or the hearer."*

In order to lay a foundation for what's coming let's try to discern some principles that occur in Paul's discourse about tongues ...

Corinthians 14:1-40 ... (1) *"Follow after charity, and desire spiritual gifts, but rather that ye may prophesy.*

(2) For he that speaketh in an unknown tongue speaketh not unto men, but unto God: for no man understandeth him; howbeit in the spirit he speaketh mysteries.

(3) But he that prophesieth speaketh unto men to edification, and exhortation, and comfort.

(4) He that speaketh in an unknown tongue edifieth himself; but he that prophesieth edifieth the church.

(5) I would that ye all spake with tongues, but rather that ye prophesied: for greater is he that prophesieth than he that speaketh with tongues, except he interpret, that the church may receive edifying.

(6) Now, brethren, if I come unto you speaking with tongues, what shall I profit you, except I shall speak to you either by revelation, or by knowledge, or by prophesying, or by doctrine?

(7) And even things without life giving sound, whether pipe or harp, except they give a distinction in the sounds, how shall it be known what is piped or harped?

(8) For if the trumpet give an uncertain sound, who shall prepare himself to the battle?

(9) So likewise ye, except ye utter by the tongue words easy to be understood, how shall it be known what is spoken? for ye shall speak into the air.

(10) There are, it may be, so many kinds of voices in the world, and none of them is without signification.

(11) Therefore if I know not the meaning of the voice, I shall be unto him that speaketh a barbarian, and he that speaketh shall be a barbarian unto me.

(12) Even so ye, forasmuch as ye are zealous of spiritual gifts, seek that ye may excel to the edifying of the church.

(13) Wherefore let him that <u>speaketh in an unknown tongue</u> pray that he may interpret.

(14) For if I pray in an unknown tongue, my spirit prayeth, but my understanding is unfruitful.

(15) What is it then? I will pray with the spirit, and I will pray with the understanding also: I will sing with the spirit, and I will sing with the understanding also.

(16) Else when thou shalt bless with the spirit, how shall he that occupieth the room of the unlearned say Amen at thy giving of thanks, seeing he understandeth not what thou sayest?

(17) For thou verily givest thanks well, but the other is not edified.

(18) I thank my God, I speak with tongues more than ye all:

(19) Yet in the church I had rather speak five words with my understanding, that by my voice I might teach others also, than ten thousand words in an unknown tongue.

(20) Brethren, be not children in understanding: howbeit in malice be ye children, but in understanding be men.

(21) In the law it is written, With men of other tongues and other lips will I speak unto this people; and yet for all that will they not hear me, saith the Lord.

(22) Wherefore tongues are for a sign, not to them that believe, but to them that believe not: but prophesying serveth not for them that believe not, but for them which believe.

(23) If therefore the whole church be come together into one place, and all speak with tongues, and there come in those that are unlearned, or unbelievers, will they not say that ye are mad?

(24) But if all prophesy, and there come in one that believeth not, or one unlearned, he is convinced of all, he is judged of all:

(25) And thus are the secrets of his heart made manifest; and so falling down on his face he will worship God, and report that God is in you of a truth.

(26) How is it then, brethren? when ye come together, every one of you hath a psalm, hath a doctrine, hath a tongue, hath a revelation, hath an interpretation. Let all things be done unto edifying.

(27) If any man speak in an unknown tongue, let it be by two, or at the most by three, and that by course; and let one interpret.

(28) But if there be no interpreter, let him keep silence in the church; and let him speak to himself, and to God.

(29) Let the prophets speak two or three, and let the other judge.

(30) If any thing be revealed to another that sitteth by, let the first hold his peace.

(31) For ye may all prophesy one by one, that all may learn, and all may be comforted.

(32) And the spirits of the prophets are subject to the prophets.

(33) For God is not the author of confusion, but of peace, as in all churches of the saints.

(34) Let your women keep silence in the churches: for it is ot permitted unto them to speak; but they are commanded to be under obedience, as also saith the law.

(35) And if they will learn any thing, let them ask their husbands at home: for it is a shame for women to speak in the church.

(36) What? came the word of God out from you? or came it unto you only?

(37) If any man think himself to be a prophet, or spiritual, let him acknowledge that the things that I write unto you are the commandments of the Lord.

(38) But if any man be ignorant, let him be ignorant.

(39) Wherefore, brethren, covet to prophesy, and forbid not to speak with tongues.

(40) Let all things be done decently and in order."

MY PERSONAL REVELATION BEGAN SEVERAL YEARS AGO ...

Evangelist Luke Medlin was preaching and he said something that I really only then began to comprehend ...

Gen. 1:26 ... *"And God said, Let us make man in our image, after our likeness: and let them have *dominion over the fish of the sea, and over the fowl of the air, and over the cattle, and over all the earth, and over every creeping thing that creepeth upon the earth."*

Gen. 1:28 ... *"And God blessed them, and God said unto them, Be fruitful, and multiply, and replenish the earth, and subdue it: and have *dominion over the fish of the sea, and over the fowl of the air, and over every living thing that moveth upon the earth."*

God not only created man in His own image, but He gave him dominion ...

Vs. 26 ... *"over all the earth"* and in vs. 28 *"over every living thing that moveth upon the earth."*

1.) *Dominion* means ... *to rule, dominate, tread down, subjugate.*

The earth is the domain of humanity. We have the power and authority over everything on the earth. EVERYTHING THAT IS ALIVE.

But we don't always fully comprehend the meaning of this. We not only have *physical* authority and power over every living thing but also spiritual authority as well. If the enemy is a created being (he is) and if he is operating on the earth (he is), then he is subject to the power and authority of the humanity made in the image of God.

When we speak, when we pray, we have the power over **everything** on the earth.

In fact, according to Matt. 16:19 ... *"And I will give unto thee the keys of the kingdom of heaven: and whatsoever thou shalt bind on earth shall be bound in heaven: and whatsoever thou shalt loose on earth shall be loosed in heaven."*

And also, Matthew 18:18 ... *"Verily I say unto you, Whatsoever ye shall bind on earth shall be bound in heaven: and whatsoever ye shall loose on earth shall be loosed in heaven."*

PRAYER IS SPEAKING OUR EARTHLY & SPIRITUAL AUTHORITY OUT LOUD ...

And affecting not only that which is on the earth, but also into the spiritual dimension of heaven or the heavens.

PRAYER MAY BE PART OF OUR DESIGN AND AUTHORITY ...

But prayer isn't always easy. Prayer depends on speaking words with faith believing. Sometimes it feels like we don't have enough faith. (Which isn't true, we've always got enough faith. Remember the Mustard Seed thing?) Sometimes because of the emotions that are produced by what is happening, we fail to express ourselves properly with words. The bottom line is for whatever reason sometimes we fail to pray like we should. Unfortunately, many factors influence us we when we pray if we allow it. But God understands our frame that we are dust. He has made provision for our weakness.

> Rom 8:26 ... KJV *"Likewise the Spirit also helpeth our infirmities: <u>for we know not what we should pray for as we ought</u>: but the Spirit itself maketh intercession for us with groanings which cannot be uttered."*

> NLT ... *"And the Holy Spirit helps us in our weakness. <u>For example, we don't know what God wants us to pray for.</u> But the Holy Spirit prays for us with groanings that cannot be expressed in words."*

> NET ... *"In the same way, the Spirit helps us in our weakness, <u>for we do not know how we should pray,</u> but the Spirit himself intercedes for us with inexpressible groanings."*

> Amplified Bible ... *"So too the (Holy) Spirit comes to our aid and bears us up in our weakness; <u>for we do not know what prayer to offer nor how to offer it worthily as we ought,</u> but the Spirit Himself goes to meet our supplication and pleads in our behalf with unspeakable yearnings and groanings too deep for utterance."*

So, when it comes to certain prayers or certain situations requiring prayer (which requires faith and the human voice) we are at a total loss as to what or how to pray. Despite the fact that God is all powerful and has all authority, He has set up a command structure upon the earth that He Himself observes. In other words, God needs your voice, your words spoken out loud in prayer so that His power can be released.

Here's the cool thing that I believe when it comes to praying in the Spirit, praying in tongues, etc. In order for God to do His will through us in prayer, He may require your faith and your voice, but He doesn't need YOU to understand what He's saying through you!

Guideposts Executive Editor Rick Hamlin

I remember walking by a storefront church once with a friend and hearing what sounded like cacophony. "They're praying in tongues," my friend told me. Really?

I can accept talking in tongues in its historical context. Back in the first century, the disciples gathered in Jerusalem after Jesus' resurrection and the Holy Spirit descended on them—veritable "flames of fire." The apostles began to speak in different tongues, languages they had no knowledge of. More importantly, they were heard in the languages they spoke.

But what I heard coming out of that storefront church? That was something else. Ecstatic utterances, people raising their hands, eyes closed. Fervent requests voiced in what frankly sounded like utter gibberish. I was tempted to react more like some of the bystanders did that first Pentecost—they figured the disciples were drunk. The Holy Spirit?

And yet, the phenomenon is well-documented and has persisted since the early days of the church. In America, its widespread practice dates back to the Azusa Street Revival in Los Angeles in 1906. The Holy Spirit descended, miracles occurred and Pentecostalism began its worldwide spread. Still, I never really knew anyone who actually spoke in tongues. It just seemed so outlandish. Imagine my surprise, then, when in the offices of Guideposts, my first boss and much beloved editor Van Varner said, "You know John speaks in tongues." John? John Sherrill? John and his wife, Elizabeth – Tibby, as she's known – were hallowed editors at Guideposts. The journalistic talent behind such classics as David Wilkerson's The Cross and the Switchblade and Corrie Ten Boom's The Hiding Place.

John was a World War II veteran and a wise, gregarious, generous man. He and Tibby met in college in Switzerland after the war. For years, he and Tibby had been members in the famously staid Episcopal Church, the same faith tradition my wife and I followed. I considered them dear colleagues and friends. But speaking in tongues? John? I labeled it as a quirk of his and paid it no more attention. Until recently.

Then, a few months after the funeral, I was at work and noticed a book of John's sitting on my shelf, "They Speak in Other Tongues". A best-seller since its release in 1964. But I had never opened it. The one book of John's I'd never read. Maybe the topic embarrassed me. Maybe I was just resistant. With some trepidation, I turned to the book. John certainly did his research. He presented case after case of eyewitness accounts. Like the scholar of ancient Arabic who recognized someone speaking an esoteric language. A language she knew well but the speaker had no knowledge of. Or a Jewish man at a religious service. He looked over his shoulder to see who was praying for him in Hebrew, only to find an Irishman who had never spoken a word of Hebrew in his life. John also made recordings of people speaking in unknown tongues and asked a few linguists to listen to them. The experts didn't recognize any specific language. But, at the same time, they could tell a recording of Tibby pretending to talk in tongues was a fake, mere gibberish. (So much for my dismissal of talking in tongues as gibberish!)

John even invited a woman who had the gift of tongues to come to his office at Guideposts. She asked if he had any special concerns. He mentioned how Tibby had been fretting over a story she was writing, near tears, the deadline looming. The woman placed her hands on John's head and prayed for Tibby, first in English and then in tongues. John didn't understand a word of it. But, as the woman spoke, he claimed he felt a wave of warmth pass from her hands into his head and swiftly down through his arms and chest. Later at home, he asked Tibby, innocently enough, how the manuscript was going. Done, she said with relief. She'd just mailed it in. The story seemed to write itself.

And then John had his own personal experience over 50 years ago in an Atlantic City hotel, at a religious convention he'd attended to investigate the phenomenon. A small group of ministers and social workers had gathered in one of the guest rooms to speak about their needs and concerns. Someone suggested they pray. John bowed his head. He listened to the voices around him and heard them dissolve into tongues. In all other instances he'd been the reporter, looking in from the outside. But now his defenses came down. A man's voice said, "I believe John wants the baptism in the Spirit." And then the group formed a circle around him. "Now the tongues swelled to a crescendo," John recalled in his book. "I opened my mouth, wondering if I too could join in, but nothing happened."

He sensed that he needed to look up. More than that, he needed to lift his hands and cry out. It was just the sort of gesture he'd always rejected as showy, but now felt compelled to do. He raised his hands and heard himself say, "Praise the Lord." Soon he too was talking and praying in tongues. As he would on occasion for the rest of his life. The key to his turnaround—this is what really hit me—was that he acknowledged that journalistic objectivity could only take you so far. Only when John lifted his head and raised his hands heavenward did he experience something new and powerful. I closed John's book. I'd heard him once say that praying in tongues was a way to say what was sometimes beyond words. And now I understood.

That loosening up, getting in touch, being "a fool for Christ." Or, to quote Paul again, "We don't know what we should pray but the Spirit itself prays for us with unexpressed groans." I still don't *pray in tongues. But I am certainly more understanding of the phenomenon. What I am sure about prayer is that there are times when we don't know what words to say—what we could possibly ask for, what we could possibly want. What a gift to have the prayer provided in words beyond understanding, knowing that they are heard by the One who understands all.*

Chapter 18

The Attitude of Prayer

Exodus 3:1-6 ... (1) *"Now Moses kept the flock of Jethro his father-in-law, the priest of Midian: and he led the flock to the backside of the desert, and came to the mountain of God, even to Horeb.*

(2) And the angel of the LORD appeared unto him in a flame of fire out of the midst of a bush: and he looked, and, behold, the bush burned with fire, and the bush was not consumed.

(3) And Moses said, I will now turn aside, and see this great sight, why the bush is not burnt.

(4) And when the LORD saw that he turned aside to see, God called unto him out of the midst of the bush, and said, Moses, Moses. And he said, Here am I.

(5) And he said, Draw not nigh hither: <u>put off thy shoes from off thy feet, for the place whereon thou standest is holy ground</u>.

(6) Moreover he said, I am the God of thy father, the God of Abraham, the God of Isaac, and the God of Jacob. And Moses hid his face; for he was afraid to look upon God."

THE IDEA OF PRAYER IS REALLY PRETTY SIMPLE ...

It is the human spirit connecting with the Spirit of God. I don't think God needs the connection as much as we do. But I do think He wants it more than we do. If that weren't true there is nothing that could keep us from prayer. NOTHING.

I am then amazed at the amount and content of the volumes of books by countless authors about prayer. The diversity of teaching on Christian prayer is almost limitless. I have several titles in my personal library, like *God Answers Prayer* by Mary Wallace (*362 pages*); *Conquest Through Prayer* by Denzil Holman (314 pages); Praying with Power by C. Peter Wagner (*231 pages*); *The Battle Plan of Prayer* by Stephen and Alex Kendrick (*249 pages*); There is the 6 volumes in one book about *Prayer* by E.M. Bounds (**622 pages**); Andrew Murray's book about prayer represents a lifetime of writings (*656 pages*); Charles Finney called the Father of Modern Revivalism 1792 – 1875 compiled four books on prayer (*558 pages*); The great pulpiteer Charles Spurgeon also contributed at least six books about prayer. (*575 pages*) along with as I have said countless other authors offering their experiences and knowledge about prayer ...

Okay one more. Richard Foster, also gives his offering on the subject of prayer simply entitled "Prayer." It has sold more than 250,000 copies and offers up these chapter titles ...

Simple Prayer, Prayer of the Forsaken, The Prayer of Tears, The Prayer of Relinquishment, Formation prayer, Covenant Prayer, The Prayer of Adoration, The Prayer of Rest, Unceasing Prayer, The Prayer of the Heart, Praying the Ordinary, Intercessory Prayer, Healing Prayer, The Prayer of Suffering, and Radical Prayer.

But throughout all these volumes of books by learned authors, although I'm sure it's in there somewhere, I don't recall a book or chapter on the subject ***the attitude of prayer***. I don't have to explain or define what attitude is. (We've all got one. And usually needs a little work).

But what I do find is that it is perhaps more important on how we approach God in prayer, than *what we say and how we say it*. The Psalmist expresses it like this ...

Psalm 34:18 ... *"The LORD is nigh unto them that are of a broken heart; and saveth such as be of a contrite spirit."*

Psalm 51:17 ... *"The sacrifices of God are a broken spirit: a broken and a contrite heart, O God, thou wilt not despise."*

I HAVE A TENDENCY TO OVER-THINK THINGS SOMETIMES ...

And so, I'm reading Exodus 3 for the umpteenth time and I see in verse five that God says to Moses, "Take off your shoes, the ground you're standing on is holy." And I stop myself and ask, "Why did Moses have to take off his shoes?" Were his sandals dirty? Were his feet any cleaner than his sandals? Was it a test of obedience? (He might step on something) Is it all the above? Or something else entirely?

So, I looked it up ... According to Gesenius Hebrew-Lexicon ... *In transferring a domain it was customary symbolically to deliver a shoe; hence casting down a shoe upon any country was a symbol of taking possession.*

Nelson's Illustrated Manner & Customs of the Bible ...

Page 481 ... *"Removing the sandal was a sign of reverence.* (Or respect)

One For Israel (*Bible based from Israel*) – *Taking Off your Shoes*

Moses and Joshua had to take off their shoes because the ground was holy, an exchange of footwear sealed the deal in Ruth, and the Psalms talk of tossing sandals at Edom... what is it with the Middle East and shoes?

Old Testament covenants are often sealed with some kind of footwear deal, and there is good reason for this. Without shoes, we are powerless. We are humbled. We are weak and incapable. We cannot go on. A soldier cannot fight without his boots, a farmer cannot plough his field, a traveler will not get very far... I once knew of someone who was robbed penniless and forced to travel through the baking desert barefoot because they also took his shoes – the anguish he must have gone through is unthinkable. God reminds the Israelites that their clothes – and their sandals – never wore out as they wandered for those 40 years in the desert, and this is a most remarkable and important provision.

By removing a shoe in the ancient Middle East, a person can be seen to be offering vulnerability – putting themselves at the mercy of the recipient. It is a statement of trust and submission.

Taking a warrior's boots and burning them is pretty much a coup d'état. It's pretty hard to come back from that. It's a resounding victory for the boot-burner (taker) and a crushing defeat for the barefooted enemy. This passage speaks to us of Yeshua's complete triumph and the contrasting powerlessness of the enemy.

I THINK I MAY BE ON TO SOMETHING ...

Before Moses could experience the supernatural presence of God, he had to give a good token of obedience and willingness to submit to His Power and authority. And I can safely say that has a lot to do with attitude.

ATTITUDE IS A WHOLE LESSON BY ITSELF ...

1 Chron. 28:9 ... KJV *"And thou, Solomon my son, know thou the God of thy father, and serve him with a perfect heart and with a willing mind: for the LORD searcheth all hearts, and understandeth all the imaginations of the thoughts: if thou seek him, he will be found of thee; but if thou forsake him, he will cast thee off for ever."*

NET ... *"And you, Solomon my son, obey the God of your father and serve him with a **submissive attitude and a willing spirit**, for the LORD examines all minds and understands every motive of one's thoughts. If you seek him, he will let you find him, but if you abandon him, he will reject you permanently."*

The *attitude of prayer* determines the access to the Holy. The access to the Holy provides grace, mercy, power, authority and intimate fellowship. Prayer must be more than asking for stuff. It must always be a display of submission, reverence, and respect for God's will and His way.

BRO. RIGGS ALWAYS TOOK HIS SHOES OFF AT THE ALTAR

My first real Pastor, Rev. James Riggs, had a habit that I noticed. At least the time I see in my mind's eye. There were several of us men praying at the church in the sanctuary and for some reason I remember Bro. Riggs taking his shoes off.

It may have been simply because his shoes were hurting his feet, but to my new convert mind I read into it that like Moses, it was a display of meekness and submission. I believed that because I could see that spirit and attitude in him.

It may be purely symbolic, but to approach God with a meek and humble attitude will get us an audience with the King of Kings!

Chapter 19

The First Principle of Addiction

Psalm 34:1-8 ... *[[A Psalm of David, when he changed his behaviour before Abimelech; who drove him away, and he departed.]] I will bless the LORD at all times: his praise shall continually be in my mouth.*

(2) My soul shall make her boast in the LORD: the humble shall hear thereof, and be glad.

(3) O magnify the LORD with me, and let us exalt his name together.

(4) I sought the LORD, and he heard me, and delivered me from all my fears.

(5) They looked unto him, and were lightened: and their faces were not ashamed.

(6) This poor man cried, and the LORD heard him, and saved him out of all his troubles.

(7) The angel of the LORD encampeth round about them that fear him, and delivereth them.

(8) **O taste and see that the LORD is good: blessed is the man that trusteth in him.**"

THE POWER OF JUST ONE TASTE

Many moons ago there was a 1972 cereal commercial featuring the quote ... *"Try it, you'll like it."* Its obvious main objective was for the average person to simply taste it, you would like it and then you would buy it. Why?

BECAUSE WE ARE CREATURES OF ADDICTION ...

From an internet article dated April 30, 2014

The definition of addiction goes like this, 'Compulsive physiological and psychological need for a habit-forming substance.' It is a state of dependence on or commitment to a habit, practice, or habit-forming substance to the extent that its cessation causes trauma, depression, panic, anxiety.

Well, here is a list of the ten most addictive things in our times:

10.) Books

> *They go hours without eating if they have a book. Their day is incomplete without reading. They get high when they smell books. They experience book hangovers.*

9.) Pessimism

> *Often referred as "negaholism." It is the addiction of always seeking out the negative aspect in everything. They tend to complain a lot, experience depression & are depressing to be around.* **The human brain has a tendency to respond more strongly to negative stimuli.**
>
> *There is no cure for an obsession with negative thinking, except maybe reading self-help literature and attending life coaching workshops ...*

8.) Music

> *While such an addiction may not prove lethal or*

dangerous, it lures us to spend a lot of time and resources on getting musical experiences. (THE WHO in concert)

It works on the same principles as cocaine.

7.) *Television*

Coach potatoes / couch surfers, bingeing, ... robs us of valuable unredeemable time and opportunities.

6.) *Shopping*

Addicts may do this to fight depression and reality. When someone indulges in shopping, the body releases endorphins that stimulate the pleasure centers of the brain.

5.) *Work*

Hence the term "workaholic." Workaholics find reasons to work and tasks to perform even when there is no real need.

4.) *Caffeine*

Caffeine stimulates the central nervous system. Excessive caffeine intake spells dependence, that can produce withdrawal symptoms like headaches, nausea, and vomiting. It is called "caffeine use disorder" and is recognized as a major health issue.

3.) *Internet / technology*

The internet addiction is still in its infancy stage. The startling fact is that the internet is slowly becoming the # 1 addiction. People have become slaves to gadgets and technology. A quote by Nassim Nicholas Taleb, "The difference between technology and slavery is that slaves are fully aware they are not free."

2.) *Alcohol*

Charles Bukowski ... "That's the problem with drinking. I thought, as I poured myself a drink. If something bad happens you drink to forget it, if something good happens you drink to celebrate it, and if nothing happens you drink to make something happen."

1.) *Drugs ...*

The most addictive drugs include heroin, cocaine, marijuana, LSD, nicotine, (and not included is Methamphetamine.) Perhaps considered the least of the previous list, nicotine becomes addictive. Of the 4,000 chemicals introduced into one's body in a drag of a cigarette, nicotine is the most addictive. Nicotine assaults the pleasure centers of the brain, and becomes hard to beat the addiction.

What Is Meth and Why Is It So Addictive?

By Becky Winslow - Submitted on August 23, 2011

Methamphetamine is a powerful stimulant that was discovered in 1919 by a Japanese scientist. It was first marketed and sold as a recreational drug, until its side effects became evident.

- *Methamphetamine provides a seemingly limitless supply of energy for the user.*
- *Meth users often report feeling superhuman with increased awareness and highly euphoric.*

The effects of Methamphetamine

- *As a stimulant methamphetamine causes a user to stay awake and alert for long periods of time. It was used during war to assist pilots to fly longer missions and ground troops to last longer on the battlefield.*
- *also known to affect the moral compass of the user.*

- *Users often feel little or no emotion when inflicting harm on others.*

Methamphetamine affects the brain

- *The effects of meth are caused by an increased production of dopamine in the brain. Dopamine is naturally produced by the body and is responsible for pleasurable feelings, ...*
- *Meth causes an abnormal amount of the drug to be released into the brain.*
- *Prolonged use of the drug damages the cells that produce dopamine and more of the drug must be taken to achieve the same result. This is a primary reason why methamphetamine is so addictive.*

Another article says ...

The first time an individual uses meth, they experience a very significant "high" off the drug. This experience becomes hard-coded into the individual's memory. Now, for the remainder of an individual's addiction, the brain will be trying to capture (or re-capture) the same positive feelings of the first use.

The problem is, NO experience is ever as intense as the first use. The brain adapts to the drug almost immediately. This means that more and more must be used each time in pursuit of the initial high.

WHAT IS THE FIRST PRINCIPLE OF ADDICTION?

All it takes is one hit, one drag, one drink, one dose, ONE TASTE of practically of anything to become addicted to it.

This is my opinion based on what I know and have experienced for myself. It is almost impossible to overcome an addiction, because it literally changes the brain chemistry. So, in my opinion, the only way to overcome a harmful and destructive addiction is to introduce a stronger, more positive addiction.

David in Psalm 34 gives us the key to overcome every other addiction known to man...

(8) *O *taste and see that the LORD is good: blessed is the man that trusteth in him.*"

* - to try the flavor, to taste, to eat a little, to perceive mentally by taste or flavor.

THE ADDICTION PSALMS

God addicts, ... are individuals who can't get enough of Him. Who can't live without Him, who can't hardly concentrate on anything else. So consumed with the desire for His presence and fellowship that everything else is secondary ...

Psalm 119:20 ... *My soul is crushed with longing after Your ordinances at all times.*

Psalm 73:25-26 ... *Whom have I in heaven but thee? and there is none upon earth that I desire beside thee.*

(26) My flesh and my heart faileth: but God is the strength of my heart, and my portion for ever.

Psalm 42:1-2 ... *(1) As the hart panteth after the water brooks, so panteth my soul after thee, O God.*

(2) My soul thirsteth for God, for the living God: when shall I come and appear before God?

Psalm 63:1-2 ... *(1) O God, thou art my God; early will I seek thee: my soul thirsteth for thee, my flesh longeth for thee in a dry and thirsty land, where no water is;*

(2) To see thy power and thy glory, so as I have seen thee in the sanctuary.

Psalm 143:6 ... *I stretch forth my hands unto thee: my soul thirsteth after thee, as a thirsty land. Selah.*

Isaiah 55:1-3 NKJV...

(1) "Ho! Everyone who thirsts, Come to the waters; And you who have no money, Come, buy and eat. Yes, come, buy wine and milk Without money and without price.

(2) Why do you spend money for what is not bread, And your wages for what does not satisfy? Listen carefully to Me, and eat what is good, And let your soul delight itself in abundance.

(3) Incline your ear, and come to Me. Hear, and your soul shall live; And I will make an everlasting covenant with you—The sure mercies of David.

WE ARE ALL ADDICTED TO SOMETHING OR SOMEONE ...

But God has provided His human creation with the safest, most satisfying, most refreshing, most powerful addiction in the universe.

RAHAB HAD HEARD SOME THINGS ABOUT GOD ...

The bible doesn't say how long the two spies were hidden in

Rahab's house, perhaps only a few hours, but that's all it took... to overcome a lifetime of idols, sinful behavior, physical and mental addictions... all she needed was a taste!

Go ahead take a taste of God ... you will be addicted!

Chapter 20

The Ineffectual Prayer of a Righteous Man

James 5:13-18 ... (13) *"Is any among you afflicted? let him pray. Is any merry? let him sing psalms.*

(14) Is any sick among you? let him call for the elders of the church; and let them pray over him, anointing him with oil in the name of the Lord:

(15) And the prayer of faith shall save the sick, and the Lord shall raise him up; and if he have committed sins, they shall be forgiven him.

(16) Confess your faults one to another, and pray one for another, that ye may be healed. **The <u>effectual fervent</u> (Strong's G1754- energeo') prayer of a righteous man availeth much.**

(17) Elias was a man subject to like passions as we are, and he prayed earnestly that it might not rain: and it rained not on the earth by the space of three years and six months.

(18) And he prayed again, and the heaven gave rain, and the earth brought forth her fruit."

VERSE 16 AGAIN ...

NKJV - *"The effective, fervent prayer of a righteous man avails much.*

NLT - *"The earnest prayer of a righteous person has great power and produces wonderful results."*

NIV - *"The prayer of a righteous person is powerful and effective."*

AMP - *"The earnest (heart-felt, continued) prayer of a righteous man makes tremendous power available – dynamic in its working."*

Synonyms (or different words that mean much the same thing) for **effectual** - *binding, capable, decisive, efficient, forcible, lawful, legal, potent, powerful, practicable, productive, qualified, strong.* (And that's just a partial list)

And antonyms are the opposite of the word you're talking about. The opposite of *effectual* is ...

- incapable, unproductive, useless, impotent, unsuccessful, ineffectual, weak.

So, the opposite of what James is talking of in chapter five, verse sixteen would sound something like this...

The Incapable (prayer), unproductive (prayer), useless (prayer), impotent (prayer), unsuccessful (prayer), ineffectual (prayer), weak (prayer) of a righteous (upright, obedient) man produces little power and limited results.

I'm not trying to change scripture but rather change our perspective of this one verse.

I really don't think that we (myself included) understand the power that is behind prayer. Yes, we have read about it. Yes, we've heard about it. Yes, we've imagined it. But few of us have ever experienced the true power of prayer.

Let's talk about the potential power of prayer just for a moment. The potential of prayer is that every person that we pray for is healed of whatever disease or affliction they are suffering from. There are only two things that stand in the way of that happening. The will of God... sometimes it's not God's will for that person to be healed at that time or for whatever reason He chooses, perhaps not at all! The second reason is our inability to use the measure of faith that God has given to every one of us. I see faith as the fuel that drives our prayers to the throne of grace. If our faith is weak or not in operation (there's no such thing as no faith), then *our prayers can become the opposite of effectual & fervent.*

Prayer is a lot like God himself. No respecter of persons. God hears the prayer of the most wicked sinner as well as the most devoted saint of God. In other words, God does not necessarily regard the prayer of the righteous more powerful than the sinner. But the prayer of the righteous can be weak and ineffective if we don't pray with faith and trust that whatever happens is the will of God.

Here is a list of people that the Bible describes as righteous or possessing righteousness ...

Abel, Noah, Joseph, Abraham, Joseph of Arimathea, Cornelius, John the Baptist & both of his parents Zacharias and Elisabeth, Simeon the Priest, and perhaps the least likely to be considered "righteous" ... Lot, Abraham's nephew.

2 Peter 2:7-8 ... 7) *"And delivered just Lot, vexed with the filthy conversation of the wicked:*

(8) (For that righteous man dwelling among them, in seeing and hearing, vexed his righteous soul from day to day with their unlawful deeds;)"

If you know the story of Lot you may consider him as the poster child for bad choices, but the Word of God describes him as being righteous. The logical conclusion is that *righteous men pray,* right? But his prayers were obviously anything but *effectual or fervent* because if it had not been for Uncle Abraham, he and his whole family would never have had the opportunity to escape the judgement of God and its destruction.

His choice of environments and activities had a direct effect upon the effectiveness of his prayers. You don't think he prayed? If two angels came to me in the evening and said God's going to totally destroy the cities in the morning, you would think he would have prayed all night long, but <u>his environment affected his prayer.</u>

NOW, LET ME ASK YOU A QUESTION ...

WOULD YOU CONSIDER THE TWELVE DISCIPLES RIGHTHEOUS?

Let's go to Matt. 17:14-21 ... (14) *"And when they were come to the multitude, there came to him a certain man, kneeling down to him, and saying,*

(15) Lord, have mercy on my son: for he is lunatick, and sore vexed: for ofttimes he falleth into the fire, and oft into the water.

(16) And I brought him to thy disciples, and they could not cure him.

(17) Then Jesus answered and said, O faithless and perverse generation, how long shall I be with you? how long shall I suffer you? bring him hither to me.

(18) And Jesus rebuked the devil; and he departed out of him: and the child was cured from that very hour.

(19) Then came the disciples to Jesus apart, and said, Why could not we cast him out?

(20) And Jesus said unto them, **Because of your unbelief***: (faithlessness, disbelief, weakness of faith) for verily I say unto you, If ye have faith as a grain of mustard seed, ye shall say unto this mountain, Remove hence to yonder place; and it shall remove; and nothing shall be impossible unto you.*

(21) Howbeit this kind goeth not out but by prayer and fasting."

Matt. 10:1 ... *"And when he had called unto him his twelve disciples, he gave them power against unclean spirits, to cast them out, and to heal all manner of sickness and all manner of disease."*

If anybody should have had faith it should have been them!

We have yet to see what God can do in this generation when the "righteous" get right and use their faith! You may pray, but are you praying effectively, decisively, powerfully, efficiently, forcibly, productively and fervently? Or are we just going through the motions?

God is looking for righteous people who will pray with faith and be obedient to His Word!

Chapter 21

The Prayer of Faith

James 5:13-15

(13) "Is any among you afflicted? let him pray. Is any merry? let him sing psalms.

(14) Is any sick among you? let him call for the elders of the church; and let them pray over him, anointing him with oil in the name of the Lord:

*(15) And **the prayer of faith** shall save the sick, and the Lord shall raise him up; and if he have committed sins, they shall be forgiven him."*

WHAT IS THE PRAYER OF FAITH?

Did James mean to distinguish it from another type of prayer or another kind of faith? (Or the popular misconception, the amount of faith.)

One thing is certain about both prayer and faith is that we cannot exist or thrive in the Kingdom of God without them both.

E.M. Bounds in his writings about prayer said this concerning prayer and faith...

Whenever a study of the principles of prayer is made, lessons concerning faith must accompany it. Faith is the essential quality in the heart of man who desires to communicate with God. He must believe and stretch out the hands of faith for that which he cannot see or prove. Prayer is actually faith claiming and taking hold of its natural, immeasurable inheritance.

Faith does the impossible because it lets God undertake for us, and nothing is impossible with God. How great-without qualification or limitation-the power of faith is!

The reality is that we must have both (prayer & faith) to accomplish the will and work of God. Some people who possess the faith never pray. And those that pray may not exercise their faith. The prayer of faith according to James releases the healing, restorative, dynamic, miracle working power of God as well as the power of salvation!

Prayer is essential because we are communicating directly with the most powerful person that we could imagine. He is not a "force," a "presence," or "a level of "consciousness" But rather the Almighty, the all-knowing, Creator and Savior of the universe!

And faith is also essential. Faith is not just believing in His ability, because He loses none of His power whether you believe it or not. But faith is actively giving God the opportunity to do what we already know He can do!

I guess what I'm trying to say is... If you believe in God's power ... Pray! And if you pray... pray with faith, conviction, and assurance that no matter what we see or don't see God's power and will are being released.

The word *faith* that James uses in his epistle literally means believe, conviction, and assurance. And Dictionary.com says the word conviction means...

A fixed or firm belief.

So, we're talking about a prayer that is prayed with no doubts, no questions, and nothing wavering.

FOR THE MOST PART ISN'T PRAYER A PETITION?

Isn't the purpose of prayer going to the ultimate Someone who alone can give you exactly what you're asking for? A doctor can give you some relief, but can he make you whole? A counselor can offer you advice that might help, but can he give you righteousness, peace, and joy? Without the asking there is no answer and without faith there is no power.

Mark 11:22-24 ... (22) *"And Jesus answering saith unto them, Have faith in God.*

*(23) For verily I say unto you, That **whosoever shall say** unto this mountain, Be thou removed, and be thou cast into the sea; and shall not doubt in his heart, but shall believe that those things which he saith shall come to pass; he shall have whatsoever he saith.*

(24) Therefore I say unto you, What things soever ye desire, when ye pray, believe that ye receive them, and ye shall have them."

Let me say this. God doesn't give you anything and everything you ask for just because you asked. When you are praying to God, you are also submitting yourself to His will.

BUT THE PRAYER OF FAITH MAY NOT ALWAYS PRODUCE THE EXPECTED RESULTS ...

According to one author I researched said the Prayer of Faith has two elements to it. *Assurance,* (that God is in control of every situation) and *submission,* (accepting the will of God no matter what.) Before I go any further let me say this. *Faith doesn't make provision for failure, but faith always accepts the will of God no matter what that may be.*

The next logical question in my mind is this, *"Is it always God's will for everyone to be healed simply because we believe he can when we anoint someone with oil and pray?"*

Let's look closely at James 5:15 again ...

"And the prayer of faith shall save the sick, and the Lord shall raise him up; and if he have committed sins, they shall be forgiven him."

We have been compelled to interpret that scripture that anyone who calls the elders together and gets anointed with oil is going to be healed, right? But what does the scripture say?

Number one: "the prayer of faith shall **save** *(Strong's G4982) the sick..."*

We have perhaps taken that scripture and implied that everyone who's prayed for with oil is *healed* (or supposed to be healed). But it does not say, *"the prayer of faith shall heal the sick ..."* James uses the word save not the word heal.

The word "heal" occurs only 40 times in the whole KJV of the Bible. It only appears 19 times in the N.T. And of those 19 times there are no less than 4 original Greek words translated as "heal." (Strong's - G2323, G2390, G1295, G2392) And none of those 4 words are the same as the word James uses for "saved" in the scripture we're talking about.

WHAT DOES THAT MEAN?

It means that scripture isn't talking about what we might think it means! Let's look at the meaning of the word *save* in James 5:15...

-to save, keep safe and sound, to rescue from danger or destruction.

to save a suffering one (from perishing), i.e. one suffering from disease, to make well, heal, restore to health

to preserve one who is in danger of destruction, to save or rescue.

Although physical healing is included in the definition the greater meaning is *safety or rescue.*

Let's look at a few stories in scripture that may illustrate dramatically what James is trying teach.

Read Daniel chapter 3 ... The Hebrews guys were commanded to bow down and worship the King's image ...

And their reply was this ...

Daniel 3:16-18 ... *(16) "Shadrach, Meshach, and Abednego, answered and said to the king, O Nebuchadnezzar, we are not careful to answer thee in this matter.*

(17) If it be so, our God whom we serve is able to deliver us from the burning fiery furnace, and he will deliver us out of thine hand, O king.

(18) But if not, be it known unto thee, O king, that we will not serve thy gods, nor worship the golden image which thou hast set up."

They weren't delivered from the fiery furnace, but they were kept safe! They displayed both assurance and submission.

How about Job ... Job 13:15 ... *"Though he slay me, yet will I trust in him: but I will maintain mine own ways before him."*

Job 19:26 ... *"And though after my skin worms destroy this body, yet in my flesh shall I see God:"*

Job understood that death is the finality for human flesh. He also understood that death wasn't final with God. That even in death he would be safe.

Esther 4:16 ... *"Go, gather together all the Jews that are present in Shushan, and fast ye for me, and neither eat nor drink three days, night or day: I also and my maidens will fast likewise; and so will I go in unto the king, which is not according to the law: and if I perish, I perish."*

PERHAPS O.T. PRAYERS OF FAITH?

And now perhaps the best N.T. example of what James would later write about.

Read John chapter 11 ... Lazarus was sick ...

John 11:4 ... *"When Jesus heard that, he said, This sickness is not unto death, but for the glory of God, that the Son of God might be glorified thereby."*

John 11:21-27 ... (21) *"Then said Martha unto Jesus, Lord, if thou hadst been here, my brother had not died."*

(22) But I know, that even now, whatsoever thou wilt ask of God, God will give it thee.

(23) Jesus saith unto her, Thy brother shall rise again.

(24) Martha saith unto him, I know that he shall rise again in the resurrection at the last day.

(25) Jesus said unto her, I am the resurrection, and the life: he that believeth in me, though he were dead, yet shall he live:

(26) And whosoever liveth and believeth in me shall never die. Believest thou this?

(27) She saith unto him, Yea, Lord: I believe that thou art the Christ, the Son of God, which should come into the world."

AND WHAT DID JAMES SAY WOULD HAPPEN?

That the prayer of faith would not only **save the sick** but also ... *"and the Lord shall **raise him up**; and if he have committed sins, they shall be forgiven him."*

Isn't forgiveness and salvation with the promise of resurrection better than physical healing?

Chapter 22

"The Lord's Prayer"

Part I

Matthew 6:9-13 ... (9) *"After this manner therefore pray ye: Our Father which art in heaven, Hallowed be thy name.*

(10) Thy kingdom come. Thy will be done in earth as it is in heaven.

(11) Give us our daily bread.

(12) And forgive us our debts, as we forgive our debtors.

(13) And lead us not into temptation, but deliver us from evil: For thine is the kingdom, and the power, and the glory, for ever. Amen."

INTRODUCTION

How many of us really know how to pray? I don't mean the mechanics of it, but real powerful, effectual, fervent prayer? I would guess many of us struggle with the idea of praying by ourselves because of a lack of self-discipline. If we had a model or a method that we could follow, would we or could we be more powerful and effective in our prayer life? When I read about prayer warriors from years ago, how they literally stayed on their knees until they received an answer from God, I ask myself, "What's the matter with me?" And if you aren't able to do it on occasion then maybe you ought to be asking yourself the same question.

The disciples observed Jesus while he was in the flesh. Prayer was not just his practice it was his lifestyle. That body, that

The Lord's Prayer Part I

humanity, that flesh, blood and bone made regular trips into the presence of the Spirit so that he could accomplish the will of God.

Traditionally Matthew 6:9-13 and again in Luke 11:1-4 are known to most of the church world as "The Lord's Prayer." But in fact, it should be called "The Disciples Prayer," because Jesus said these words in response to their request in Luke 11:1 ...

*"And it came to pass, that, as he was praying in a certain place, when he ceased, one of his disciples said unto him, **Lord, teach us to pray**, as John also taught his disciples."*

If you would allow me a little speculation, I think most if not all of them already knew something about prayer, but if I could paraphrase that question, I think it might sound a little like, "Jesus, teach us how to pray like <u>you</u> pray." "Jesus, teach us how to pray so that we can do the things you do." "Jesus, how do we accomplish the same level of intimacy with the Spirit of God as you do?" No matter how you slice it, dice it, cut it, or stack it the disciples wanted to know how to pray not only with power and authority but with effectiveness as well.

Even after the mini lesson on prayer and spending 3 ½ years in direct contact with him, on one of the most important nights in his ministry, Jesus while praying with his disciples in the garden relates this...

Read Matthew 26:36-46 *"Could you not tarry with me one hour?"*

Tithing our time... 2 hours and 40 minutes each day??? (Realistic?)

What if we could train or teach ourselves to **pray one hour a day**?

Would it transform us?

Would it increase our faith?

Would it have an impact on my home, my family, my church, my city, my country's government?

WE NEED TO LEARN HOW TO PRAY!

James 5:16 ... "*Confess your faults one to another, and pray one for another, that ye may be healed. The effectual fervent (to effect – G1754 energeo) prayer of a righteous man availeth much.*"

Anything we do without prayer is doomed to fail. Anything we do with prayer, may not change what we're praying for or about, but it will change the one doing the praying. If we are truly praying for God's will. Sometimes God doesn't want to change our situation as much as he wants to change us.

We must learn to pray not just with faith, not just with power, not just effectively, but with a willingness to let God change us and mold us and shape us into his image.

The Plan – Using the "Lord's Prayer" we are going to learn a method how to pray for one hour.

Chapter 23

The Primary Purpose of Prayer

The Secondary Purpose of Evil

Isa. 13:11 ... "*And I will punish the world for their evil, and the wicked for their iniquity; and I will cause the arrogancy of the proud to cease, and will lay low the haughtiness of the terrible.*"

Isa. 31:1-2 ... (1) "*Woe to them that go down to Egypt for help; and stay on horses, and trust in chariots, because they are many; and in horsemen, because they are very strong; but they look not unto the Holy One of Israel, neither seek the LORD!*

(2) Yet he also is wise, and will bring evil, and will not call back his words: but will arise against the house of the evildoers, and against the help of them that work iniquity."

Isa. 33:15-17 ... (15) "*He that walketh righteously, and speaketh uprightly; he that despiseth the gain of oppressions, that shaketh his hands from holding of bribes, that stoppeth his ears from hearing of blood, and shutteth his eyes from seeing evil;*

(16) He shall dwell on high: his place of defence shall be the munitions of rocks: bread shall be given him; his waters shall be sure.

(17) Thine eyes shall see the king in his beauty: they shall behold the land that is very far off."

Isa. 45:7 ... *"I form the light, and create darkness: I make peace, <u>and create evil</u>: I the LORD do all these things."*

WHY DO WE PRAY?

I don't think I need to define evil. We see evidence of its existence almost every day. Rather I would ask the question, *"What is the purpose of evil?"* And also, *"what does evil have to do with prayer?"*

Let's try to deal with the first question ... What is the purpose of evil? Well at first glance I would say these things with qualification. The purpose of evil is ...

- Not to offer the world a balanced society.
- Not to offer a moral choice to the individual.
- Not to scare us into the kingdom of God.
- Not to punish us for wrong or lazy behavior.
- Not to push God's people to pray.

All those statements perhaps have certain merit and possibly a secondary reason that God allows evil to exist. But I am positive it isn't the primary reason for prayer.

I know what the Lord's Prayer says, *"...but deliver us from evil..."* And prayer is definitely a weapon of our warfare in our spiritual experience, but it's not the primary reason for prayer.

- June 12, 1775, prayer was made at the start of the American Revolutionary War
- During the Civil War, President Abraham Lincoln declared April 30, 1863, as a day of national prayer.

- During World War I President Woodrow Wilson proclaimed May 30, 1918, to be a day of prayer.

- A day of prayer was called on May 26, 1940, for Britain as the trapped British Expeditionary Force faced annihilation by the Nazi war machine on the beaches of Dunkirk.

- In April of 1970, President Richard Nixon had the nation observe a Day of Prayer for Apollo 13 astronauts.

- in the hurricane season of 2017, President Trump had reason to call a special day of prayer on September 3.

Prayer may be appropriate and powerful when evil or sudden destruction comes but it's NOT the primary purpose of prayer.

Since God created us and He created prayer, then He knows how we usually approach prayer. God knows that we are by in large reactionary in prayer. In other words, the only time we REALLY pray is when it seems evil is in charge. But that isn't the primary purpose for prayer.

The purpose of prayer was not meant to be an emotional response to evil, (although God may well use it for that very purpose), but the primary purpose of prayer is meant to connect us to the Almighty, the Creator, our Father in intimate personal fellowship. The truth is that very few of us pray because of the simple joy of God's fellowship.

Through listening to a few of the modern-day prophets of God we can see clearly that evil is NOT the primary purpose of prayer. Yes, God uses evil to prompt His people to pray in a more fervent manner, but we should already be praying fervently!

What would we have done if Donald Trump would have been declared the winner on Nov. 3, 2020? We would have settled back into our comfortable routines and waited for Bro. Trump to fix everything, right?

But God wants more for us! He wants us to seek Him not a man! He wants us to seek His face, not a political problem solver! He wants us to seek Him in the good and the evil! He wants us to seek Him because we love Him more than this life!

That's the primary purpose of prayer!

Chapter 24

The Seed Principle of Prayer

Galatians 6:6-10 ... NKJV (6) *"Let him who is taught the word share in all good things with him who teaches.*

(7) Do not be deceived, God is not mocked; for whatever a man sows, that he will also reap.

(8) For he who sows to his flesh will of the flesh reap corruption, but he who sows to the Spirit will of the Spirit reap everlasting life.

(9) And let us not grow weary while doing good, for in due season we shall reap if we do not lose heart.

(10) Therefore, as we have opportunity, let us do good to all, especially to those who are of the household of faith."

Psalm 126:1-6 ... KJV *[[A Song of degrees.]] When the LORD turned again the captivity of Zion, we were like them that dream.*

(2) Then was our mouth filled with laughter, and our tongue with singing: then said they among the heathen, The LORD hath done great things for them.

(3) The LORD hath done great things for us; whereof we are glad.

(4) Turn again our captivity, O LORD, as the streams in the south.

(5) They that sow in tears shall reap in joy.

(6) He that goeth forth and weepeth, bearing precious seed,

shall doubtless come again with rejoicing, bringing his sheaves with him."

NOTHING GROWS OR IS REPRODUCED WITHOUT SEEDS

This Biblical principle is that nothing whether physical or spiritual is ever realized or comes to pass without the sowing of seeds. Seeds represent both potential and promise. So, without the sowing of seeds there is no potential and no promises.

<u>Everything that God creates or establishes</u>
<u>is based on the seed principle.</u>

In Genesis chapter one everything God created on the Earth was created with the potential of reproduction by the power of seeds ...

Gen 1:11 ... *"And God said, Let the earth bring forth grass, the herb yielding seed, and the fruit tree yielding fruit after his kind, whose seed is in itself, upon the earth: and it was so."*

And that included the rest of His creation, even man ...

Gen. 3:15 ... *"And I will put enmity between thee and the woman, <u>and between thy seed and her seed</u>; it shall bruise thy head, and thou shalt bruise his heel."*

Specifically, the Word mentions ... The seed of Abraham, The seed of Israel /Jacob, The seed of David, the seed of Aaron, the seed of Zadok ...

Everything that is physical (the birds and the bees) operate under the fixed principle of seeds!

AND EVERYTHING SPIRITUAL OPERATES UNDER THE FIXED PRINCIPLE OF SEEDS!

MATTHEW 13 COULD BE CALLED THE "SEED" CHAPTER

Vs. 1-23 – *The Parable of the Sower*

Is not a story just about farmers, sowing and soil. It is a story to illustrate the principle and potential of the seeds. The seed is the Word of God. The power, potential and promises of God are only released if seeds are sown into the soil of men's hearts and minds.

The Word of God is spiritual and has power to grow and reproduce but only if it is sowed or planted!

Vs. 24-30 – *The Parable of the Wheat & Tares / vs. 36-43 explanation*

It's not a story about wheat and "weeds" (my word) which look very much like the wheat itself, but isn't. It is a story about how the influence of either good or evil is established. It is also a story about how either good or evil can be perpetuated simply by a "seed."

Matt. 13:36-43 ... (36) *"Then Jesus sent the multitude away, and went into the house: and his disciples came unto him, saying, Declare unto us the parable of the tares of the field.*

(37) He answered and said unto them, <u>He that soweth the good seed is the Son of man</u>;

(38) The field is the world; <u>the good seed are the children of the kingdom; but the tares are the children of the wicked one</u>;

(39) <u>The enemy that sowed them is the devil; the harvest is the end of the world; and the reapers are the angels</u>.

(40) As therefore the tares are gathered and burned in the fire; so shall it be in the end of this world.

(41) The Son of man shall send forth his angels, and they shall

gather out of his kingdom all things that offend, and them which do iniquity;

(42) And shall cast them into a furnace of fire: there shall be wailing and gnashing of teeth.

(43) Then shall the righteous shine forth as the sun in the kingdom of their Father. Who hath ears to hear, let him hear."

Prov. 11:21 ... *"Though hand join in hand, the wicked shall not be unpunished: <u>but the seed of the righteous shall be delivered</u>."*

Psalm 37:28 ... *"For the LORD loveth judgment, and forsaketh not his saints; they are preserved for ever: <u>but the seed of the wicked shall be cut off</u>."*

The enemy has the ability to sow seeds of fear, doubt, unbelief, etc. He doesn't have to do the actual work He just sows the seed and it grows! <u>The devil he is a farmer</u>. He sows his "seed" among the wheat and it can also produce tares and sometimes they grow together. Both are produced from "seeds" sowed to produce influence, or a desired result.

Vs. 31-32 – <u>*Faith is a Mustard Seed*</u> – And Mark 4:31

The seed principle of faith is that everyone ... is given a "measure" (or a "seed") of faith. And the secondary principle is this. All you need is a single (smallest) seed of faith to produce great results. Jesus illustrates this in John 12:24 ...

"Verily, verily, I say unto you, Except <u>a corn of wheat</u> fall into

the ground and die, it abideth alone: but if it die, it bringeth forth much fruit."

NKJV ... "Most assuredly, I say to you, unless _a grain of wheat falls into the ground and dies, it remains alone; but if it dies, it produces much grain._"

New Living Translation ... "I tell you the truth, unless _a kernel of wheat_ is planted in the soil and dies, it remains alone. But its death will produce many new kernels—a plentiful harvest of new lives."

Amplified Bible ... "I assure you, most solemnly I tell you, unless _a grain of wheat_ falls into the earth and dies, it remains [just one grain; never becomes more but lives] by itself alone. But if it dies, it produces many others and yields a rich harvest."

PRAYER IS A SEED ...

If everything in the natural operates through the seed principle, then it seems to be sound doctrine and belief that everything that is spiritual also operates by the seed principle.

And as such, prayer operates under the fixed principle of sowing and reaping. Most all of us operate in prayer wanting the answer, wanting the miracle, wanting the healing, wanting the blessing instantly the second it comes out of our mouth, but if prayer is a seed, then it operates under the same fixed rule as everything else in creation.

So, ask yourself...

Are you sowing the seeds of prayer?

What can one seed of prayer yield?

What is the potential and the power of just one prayer?

I don't know or remember who said it ...

Little prayer / little power ... Much prayer / much power

Pastor / Author Mark Batterson - *"Each prayer is like a seed that gets planted in the ground. It disappears for a season, but it eventually bears fruit that blesses future generations. In fact, our prayers bear fruit forever."*

Every time we pray we must embrace the idea ... "I am sowing seeds!" The natural and spiritual seed principle proves that one prayer has the power and potential to produce more fruit than we can comprehend. Don't let the enemy sow his seeds of doubt, fear or unbelief in your heart! Pray without ceasing!

Chapter 25

"The Lord's Prayer"

Part II

Matthew 6:9-13 ... (9) *"After this manner therefore pray ye: Our Father which art in heaven, Hallowed be thy name.*

(10) Thy kingdom come. Thy will be done in earth as it is in heaven.

(11) Give us this day our daily bread.

(12) And forgive us our debts, as we forgive our debtors.

(13) And lead us not into temptation, but deliver us from evil: For thine is the kingdom, and the power, and the glory, for ever. Amen."

INTRODUCTION

Prayer is something every child of God should practice on a daily basis. But we mistakenly think that somehow prayer is something that should come naturally to us. Well, if that were the case why did the closest followers, the hand-picked twelve, have to say this to Jesus?

"And it came to pass, that, as he was praying in a certain place, when he ceased, one of his disciples said unto him, Lord, teach us to pray, as John also taught his disciples." —Luke 11:1

DISCIPLINE IS A FOUR-LETTER WORD ...

In his book *Celebration of Discipline*, Richard J. Foster says this about prayer...

Prayer catapults us onto the frontier of the spiritual life. Of all the Spiritual Disciplines prayer is the most central because it ushers us into perpetual communion with the Father. It is the discipline of prayer that brings us into the deepest and highest work of the human spirit. Real prayer is life creating and life changing.

To pray is to change. Prayer is the central avenue God uses to transform us. (page 33)

If prayer is described as a "discipline," then that means it doesn't come naturally to the flesh. It is a behavior, practice, habit, etc. that we adopt through a willful and conscious act.

The flesh must willingly bow to the spirit and do what it is not able to do otherwise. Remember what Jesus said to the sleepy guys in the garden... Matthew 26: 41...

"Watch and pray, that ye enter not into temptation: **the** *(human)* **spirit indeed is willing, but the flesh is weak."**

So effective, fervent, passionate, powerful prayer is something we gain by discipline and training our flesh to submit to the will of the Spirit.

THE LORD'S PRAYER IS AN OUTLINE

History tells us that in the first century, Jewish Rabbis (teachers), would provide an outline to teach their pupils or disciples in topics that pertained to truth. Therefore, when the disciples asked Jesus to teach them to pray, he offered them not just something to repeat or memorize, they were to use it as an outline or model on how to pray.

Brad Young, author of the book *The Jewish Background to the Lord's Prayer*, points out that this is exactly what Jesus taught the disciples and is illustrated in Acts 1:14.

"These all continued with one accord in prayer and supplication, with the women, and Mary the mother of Jesus, and with his brethren."

Young says that the original Greek does not read *"in prayer,"* rather the verse actually should read, *"These continued with one accord in **the prayer** and supplication..."* He adds that ancient literature often refers to the Lord's Prayer as **The Prayer**. Some certain writings include prayers of early Christians which are based on the Lord's Prayer model and require about an hour to pray through.

We have convinced ourselves that prayer has to be spontaneous, but prayer is a discipline, not some shoot from the hip shotgun blast, but it is a trained sniper with a single purpose and direction.

THE FIRST TEN MINUTES

If your goal is to pray for one hour a day, or one total hour, using the Lord's prayer as a model then let's see how it begins...

(9) ..."*Our Father which art in heaven, Hallowed be thy name.*"

The word "hallowed" simply means to sanctify or set apart. We need to recognize who we are praying to. You think God automatically knows who you're talking to? He might if you call him by his name. That's what gets you more of His attention. By using His name, we focus our attention and love on the proper one. (His name's not Bubba)

THE PRAYER begins and ends in praise. Before we ask for anything, before we whine about everything, before we get distracted, the first thing we should do anytime we come to God in prayer is praise his name! This is the principle that the psalmist inserts into Psalm 100:4 ...

*"Enter into his gates with thanksgiving, and into his courts with praise: be thankful unto him and bless **his name**."* —Psalm 100:4

Psalm 8:1 says... *"O Lord our Lord, how excellent is **thy name** in all the earth! Who has set thy glory above the heavens."*

Psalm 148:13 ... *"Let them praise **the name of the Lord**: for **his name** alone is excellent; his glory is above the earth and heaven."*

Psalm 124:8 ... *"Our help is in the name of the Lord, who made heaven and earth."*

Proverbs 18:10 ... *"The name of the Lord is a strong tower: the righteous runneth into it and is safe."*

Isaiah 59:19 ... *"So shall they fear **the name of the Lord** from the west, and his glory from the rising of the sun. When the enemy shall come in like a flood, the spirit of the Lord shall lift up a standard against him."*

Micah 4:5 ... *"For all the people will walk every one in the **name** of his god, and we will walk in **the name of the Lord** our God for ever and ever."*

But what is the name that we should use? After all God had a lot of "names" in the O.T. There was Jevovah-Tsidkenu (The Lord our Righteousness), Jevovah-M'Kaddesh (The Lord who Sanctifies), Jehovah-Shalom (The Lord our Peace), Jehovah-Shammah (The Lord is There), Jehovah-Rophe' (The Lord who Heals), Jehovah-Jireh (The Lord our Provider), Jehovah-Rohi (The Lord my Shepherd) and Jehovah-Nissi (The Lord our Banner). It could get kind of confusing. Let's not get too stressed trying to remember all those compound names. There's just one name we need to remember... JESUS!

Acts 4:10 &12 says ... *"Be it known unto you all, and to all the* *people of Israel, that by **the name of Jesus of Nazareth**, whom ye crucified, whom God raised from the dead, even by him doth this man stand here before you whole.*

*(12) Neither is salvation in any other: for there is **none other name** given among men, whereby we must be saved."*

Philippians 2:9-10... (9) *"Wherefore God also hath highly exalted him, and **given him a name which is above every name**:*

*(10) "That at **the name of Jesus** every knee should bow, of things in heaven, and things in earth, and things under the earth;*

(11) And every tongue confess that Jesus Christ is Lord, to the glory of God the Father."

To make a practical, consistent application to our prayer time, we should always open our prayer time with PRAISE. And not just any PRAISE, but praise which makes the name of Jesus the first thing we mention. That's who you've come to talk to isn't? You want to begin by getting his attention? What did Bartimaeus do?

"Jesus, thou son of David, have mercy on me!"

LET'S FOLLOW THE MODEL

Listen saints, we're trying to follow a model here. The model, if used correctly produces effectual, fervent, powerful prayers that change us, not just change our circumstance. If we want to properly enter into His presence and before we ask him for anything... tough to do... we need to "hallow" his name!

You can sing, read or quote these scriptures, play some praise music, but take the time to open with the praise that is due his name!

I Chron. 16:29 ... **"Give unto the Lord the glory due unto his name:** *bring an offering, and come before him: worship the Lord in the beauty of holiness."*

Psalm 29:2 ... **"Give unto the Lord the glory due unto his name:** *worship the Lord in the beauty of holiness."*

Psalm 96:8 ... **"Give unto the Lord the glory due unto his name:** *bring an offering, and come into his courts."*

THE FIRST TEN MINUTES ...

PRAISE HIS NAME!

Chapter 26

"The Servant's Prayer"

Daniel 9:16-19 ... *(16) O Lord, according to all thy righteousness, I beseech thee, let thine anger and thy fury be turned away from thy city Jerusalem, thy holy mountain: because for our sins, and for the iniquities of our fathers, Jerusalem and thy people are become a reproach to all that are about us.*

(17) Now therefore, O our God, hear **the prayer of thy servant***, and his supplications, and cause thy face to shine upon thy sanctuary that is desolate, for the Lord's sake.*

(18) O my God, incline thine ear, and hear; open thine eyes, and behold our desolations, and the city which is called by thy name: for we do not present our supplications before thee for our righteousnesses, but for thy great mercies.

(19) O Lord, hear; O Lord, forgive; O Lord, hearken and do; defer not, for thine own sake, O my God: for thy city and thy people are called by thy name."

Even in the Church, believe it or not, we can get caught up or hung up on titles and positions. Our culture thrives on the idea of being the best, the highest, the greatest, the champion. But if we want to reach God in prayer, we must come to him in the proper attitude and mind set.

It's true that we are kings and priests unto God. It's true we are his bride and can ask anything in his name. It's true that we are unique and have direct access to His power and authority. But in the kingdom of God the least shall be the greatest, the weakest become the strongest, the last become the first, the king and the priest become servants. So according to the word of God a servant is the highest rank or position in the kingdom of God.

LET'S FACE IT PEOPLE, A SERVANT ISN'T A TOP CAREER CHOICE

You probably won't see "servant" on too many high school career choice surveys. And when we think of the Biblical definition of servant, which amounted to being a slave and made to do whatever their master wanted them to do. I mean come on who would want to be a slave, a servant, without the ability to do whatever and whenever you wanted to do it.

The True Story of Servants
By ADRIAN LEE

HIDDEN away below stairs an army of people were once the vital cogs that kept the home of the wealthy running smoothly. For little reward these men and women toiled from before dawn until after dusk.

At the turn of the 20th century when the population of Britain was only 36 million there were 1.5 million servants. That is more than worked on the land or in factories.

In the big country houses or the great London mansions servants were crammed into shared bedrooms and beds with no bathroom or lavatory facilities. They wore white gloves to serve at table to conceal their grubby hands.

Apparently, nothing was considered too menial and records

show that servants' duties included ironing shoelaces and cutting their masters' toenails.

Despite the awful wages and conditions competition for places was fierce. In Edwardian times going into service was frequently the only alternative to near starvation. Girls worked part-time for two years to buy the uniform necessary to secure a job because service offered a roof over their heads and regular meals.

Yet while their employers dined on nine-course meals costing up to six times a maid's annual wage, employees were treated to the leftovers in the kitchen. Servants worked 17-hour days with time off limited to church on Sunday morning and one afternoon a week.

Invisibility and segregation were part of their job. In some stately homes such as Petworth in West Sussex hidden passages kept servants separate from family members to spare them the embarrassment of encountering this under-class. Servants were expected to "know their place."

Margaret Powell, a former servant who died in 1984, recalled in her memoirs: "I was confined to the basement, the backstairs and the miserable attic room that I shared with another maid and which was so cold in winter that the ice froze in the jugs of water we used for washing.

"I got up at 5:30 a.m. to clean the fireplaces and front steps, polish the shoes and boots of everyone in the household. I was shouted at by the harridan of a cook and treated like some sort of sub-human by my employers who found fault with everything I did."

In addition to wearing uniforms servants were expected to have matching hairstyles. Bizarrely in another stripping away of identity they were sometimes given generic names. Historical archives reveal that countless footmen were called William, Henry or James, which were considered "acceptable" names. A favourite maid's name was Sarah.

Such was the life of a servant.

THE KINGDOM OF GOD ...
RULERS WHO SERVE OR SERVANTS WHO RULE?

Mark 10:35-45 - James and John wanted a position...

(35) *"And James and John, the sons of Zebedee, come unto him, saying, Master, we would that thou shouldest do for us whatsoever we shall desire.*

(36) *And he said unto them, What would ye that I should do for you?*

(37) *They said unto him, Grant unto us that we may sit, one on thy right hand, and the other on thy left hand, in thy glory.*

(38) *But Jesus said unto them, Ye know not what ye ask: can ye drink of the cup that I drink of? and be baptized with the baptism that I am baptized with?*

(39) *And they said unto him, We can. And Jesus said unto them, Ye shall indeed drink of the cup that I drink of; and with the baptism that I am baptized withal shall ye be baptized:*

(40) *But to sit on my right hand and on my left hand is not mine to give; but it shall be given to them for whom it is prepared.*

(41) *And when the ten heard it, they began to be much displeased with James and John.*

(42) *But Jesus called them to him, and saith unto them, Ye know that they which are accounted to rule over the Gentiles exercise lordship over them; and their great ones exercise authority upon them.*

(43) *But so shall it not be among you: but whosoever will be great among you, shall be your minister:*

(44) *And whosoever of you will be the chiefest, shall be servant of all.*

(45) For even the Son of man came not to be ministered unto, but to minister, and to give his life a ransom for many."

THE SERVANT'S PRAYER

I Kings 8:27-30 ... Solomon was the King

(27) But will God indeed dwell on the earth? behold, the heaven and heaven of heavens cannot contain thee; how much less this house that I have builded?

(28) Yet have thou respect unto the prayer of thy servant, and to his supplication, O LORD my God, to hearken unto the cry and to the prayer, which thy servant prayeth before thee to day:

(29) That thine eyes may be open toward this house night and day, even toward the place of which thou hast said, My name shall be there: that thou mayest hearken unto the prayer which thy servant shall make toward this place.

(30) And hearken thou to the supplication of thy servant, and of thy people Israel, when they shall pray toward this place: and hear thou in heaven thy dwelling place: and when thou hearest, forgive."

But it wasn't the king's prayer, it was the servant's prayer!

Nehemiah 1:4-6, 10-11 ... Nehemiah was the Governor

(4) And it came to pass, when I heard these words, that I sat down and wept, and mourned certain days, and fasted, and prayed before the God of heaven,

(5) And said, I beseech thee, O LORD God of heaven, the great and terrible God, that keepeth covenant and mercy for them that love him and observe his commandments:

(6) Let thine ear now be attentive, and thine eyes open, that

thou mayest hear **the prayer of thy servant**, which I pray before thee now, day and night, for the children of Israel thy servants, and confess the sins of the children of Israel, which we have sinned against thee: both I and my father's house have sinned.

Dropping down to verse 10 ...

(10) Now these are thy servants and thy people, whom thou hast redeemed by thy great power, and by thy strong hand.

(11) O Lord, I beseech thee, let now thine ear be attentive to the prayer of thy servant, and to the prayer of thy servants, who desire to fear thy name: and prosper, I pray thee, thy servant this day, and grant him mercy in the sight of this man. For I was the king's cupbearer."

But it wasn't the governor's prayer it was a servant's prayer!

AND DANIEL WAS ONE OF THE THREE MOST POWERFUL PEOPLE UNDER THE KING

Technically, he was a ruler, a chief, an overseer of all Babylon and Persia under the King himself. He had power, position, authority, and even a measure of independence, **but when he prayed, He became the servant of the most high!**

We must become kings and priests with a servant's mentality to do whatever he wants us to do!

Chapter 27

The Prayer of Pursuit & Recovery

I Samuel 30:1 ... NKJV (1) *"Now it happened, when David and his men came to Ziklag, on the third day, that the Amalekites had invaded the South and Ziklag, attacked Ziklag and burned it with fire,*

(2) and had taken captive the women and those who were there, from small to great; they did not kill anyone, but carried them away and went their way.

(3) So David and his men came to the city, and there it was, burned with fire; and their wives, their sons, and their daughters had been taken captive.

(4) Then David and the people who were with him lifted up their voices and wept, until they had no more power to weep.

(5) And David's two wives, Ahinoam the Jezreelitess, and Abigail the widow of Nabal the Carmelite, had been taken captive.

(6) Now David was greatly distressed, for the people spoke of stoning him, because the soul of all the people was grieved, every man for his sons and his daughters. But David strengthened himself in the LORD his God.

(7) Then David said to Abiathar the priest, Ahimelech's son, "Please bring the ephod here to me." And Abiathar brought the ephod to David.

*(8) **So David inquired of the LORD, saying, "Shall I pursue***

this troop? Shall I overtake them?" And He answered him, "Pursue, for you shall surely overtake them and without fail recover all."

(9) So David went, he and the six hundred men who were with him, and came to the Brook Besor, where those stayed who were left behind.

(10) But David pursued, he and four hundred men; for two hundred stayed behind, who were so weary that they could not cross the Brook Besor.

(11) Then they found an Egyptian in the field, and brought him to David; and they gave him bread and he ate, and they let him drink water.

(12) And they gave him a piece of a cake of figs and two clusters of raisins. So when he had eaten, his strength came back to him; for he had eaten no bread nor drunk water for three days and three nights.

(13) Then David said to him, "To whom do you belong, and where are you from?" And he said, "I am a young man from Egypt, servant of an Amalekite; and my master left me behind, because three days ago I fell sick.

(14) "We made an invasion of the southern area of the Cherethites, in the territory which belongs to Judah, and of the southern area of Caleb; and we burned Ziklag with fire."

(15) And David said to him, "Can you take me down to this troop?" So he said, "Swear to me by God that you will neither kill me nor deliver me into the hands of my master, and I will take you down to this troop."

(16) And when he had brought him down, there they were, spread out over all the land, eating and drinking and dancing, because of all the great spoil which they had taken from the land of the Philistines and from the land of Judah.

(17) Then David attacked them from twilight until the evening

of the next day. Not a man of them escaped, except four hundred young men who rode on camels and fled.

(18) So David recovered all that the Amalekites had carried away, and David rescued his two wives.

(19) And nothing of theirs was lacking, either small or great, sons or daughters, spoil or anything which they had taken from them; David recovered all.

(20) >>>>Then<<<< David took all the flocks and herds they had driven before those other livestock, and said, "This is David's spoil."

(21) Now David came to the two hundred men who had been so weary that they could not follow David, whom they also had made to stay at the Brook Besor. So they went out to meet David and to meet the people who were with him. And when David came near the people, he greeted them.

(22) Then all the wicked and worthless men of those who went with David answered and said, "Because they did not go with us, we will not give them any of the spoil that we have recovered, except for every man's wife and children, that they may lead them away and depart."

(23) But David said, "My brethren, you shall not do so with what the LORD has given us, who has preserved us and delivered into our hand the troop that came against us.

(24) "For who will heed you in this matter? But as his part is who goes down to the battle, so shall his part be who stays by the supplies; they shall share alike."

(25) So it was, from that day forward; he made it a statute and an ordinance for Israel to this day."

I ALWAYS BELIEVED I WON THE TEN MILLION

FROM PUBLISHER'S CLEARINGHOUSE ...

Yep, you'll never convince me otherwise. But I've also have come to believe something else in the last several years and it has to do with the enemy.

John 10:10 ... NKJV *"The thief does not come except to steal, and to kill, and to destroy. I have come that they may have life, and that they may have it more abundantly."*

So, whatever the enemy can't kill, He destroys (if he can't have it nobody will), and what he can't destroy he steals. And he will steal anything and everything he considers even remotely precious to you. The point is, what will you let him steal from you? The thing is, the enemy isn't nearly as powerful as you think he is, he's just very brass about stealing somebody else's stuff.

During a time when I worked as a maintenance man at a local church, a family that lived right across the street had their four-wheeler and trailer stolen 15' from one of the busiest streets in the city and right next to their house!

And you're more powerful in prayer than you think you are. What God has given you, He means for you to keep it. And what the enemy has stolen isn't always recovered simply because you haven't prayed for its recovery.

Yeah, I know, "stuff" can be replaced, but family can't be replaced. This story openly reveals how important family is to God. And that in a culture where wives / women had very little legal standing. In some ways they were treated as property not equals. Like some of those guys probably said something like, ...

"I can get another wife, I can have more kids, etc. So why should I risk dying in battle to get back what I can get somewhere else without as much risk?"

But I like to believe that David probably said something like, *"Hey! That's my wife you took! Those are my children you stole! That's my stuff that God gave me!"*

And if God gave it to me, if I pray, He will do one of two things: 1.) Replace what was stolen. Or 2) allow me to pursue the enemy and recover everything that was lost. In fact, He may also allow me to "spoil the enemy!" To take from the enemy more than what he took from me.

You ever wonder why evil men and women are so wealthy? Ever wonder why evil never runs out of money and resources? It's not because he works hard for his money!

Practically everything he has he's stolen from somebody else.

There are times when God is willing to restore what the enemy has taken simply because you ask, then you just might end up with more than when you started out with... because you prayed the prayer of Pursuit & Recovery!

Job 12:19 ... NKJV *"He leads princes away plundered, And overthrows the mighty."*

Col. 2:15 ... KJV *"And having spoiled principalities and powers, he made a shew of them openly, triumphing over them in it."*

Luke 11:21-22 ... NKJV (21) *"When a strong man, fully armed, guards his own palace, his goods are in peace.*

(22) "But when a stronger than he comes upon him and overcomes him, he takes from him all his armor in which he trusted, and divides his spoils.

Jeremiah 51:53 ... KJV *"Though Babylon should mount up to heaven, and though she should fortify the height of her strength, yet from me shall spoilers come unto her, saith the LORD."*

Exo. 12:36 ... KJV *"And the LORD gave the people favour in the sight of the Egyptians, so that they lent unto them such things as they required. And they spoiled the Egyptians."*

1 Sam. 17:53 ... *"And the children of Israel returned from chasing after the Philistines, and they spoiled their tents."*

Eze. 39:9 ... KJV (9) *"And they that dwell in the cities of Israel shall go forth, and shall set on fire and burn the weapons, both the shields and the bucklers, the bows and the arrows, and the handstaves, and the spears, and they shall burn them with fire seven years:*

(10) So that they shall take no wood out of the field, neither cut down any out of the forests; for they shall burn the weapons with fire: and they shall spoil those that spoiled them, and rob those that robbed them, saith the Lord GOD."

WHAT HAS THE ENEMY STOLEN FROM YOU?

Has he stolen your spouse?

Has he stolen your children?

Has he stolen your blessing or your birthright?

Has he stolen your prayer life?

Has stolen your joy / peace?

Has he stolen your promises?

Has he stolen ... _____ ?

Maybe it's time to pray the prayer of pursuit & recovery.

"MR. PRESIDENT, YOU SHALL RECOVER ALL!"

To make a long story short, during Donald Trump's first term, he had an advisory board made up of some Pastors, Teachers, & Evangelists. And on one short YouTube video they were gathered around him in the Oval office laying on hands and praying for him.

At the end, one of the women stepped forward and prophesied over him saying the words ...

"MR. PRESIDENT, YOU SHALL RECOVER ALL!"

The prayer principle includes that when you pursue God in prayer you will not only get more of God but He may also allow you to recover everything (and spoil) what the enemy has stolen from us!

Chapter 28

"The Lord's Prayer"

Part III

Matthew 6:9-13 / Luke 11:2-4

(9) "After this manner therefore pray ye: "Our Father which art in *heaven, Hallowed be thy name.*

(10) *Thy kingdom come. Thy will be done in earth as it is in heaven.*

(11) *Give us this day our daily bread.*

(12) *And forgive us our debts, as we forgive our debtors.*

(13) *And lead us not into temptation, but deliver us from evil: For thine is the kingdom, and the power, and the glory, for ever Amen.*

INTRODUCTION

What we call the Lord's Prayer is what Christ gave to his disciples in response to the request in Luke 11:1b where it says...

"Lord, teach us to pray, as John also taught his disciples."

Their request reflects every generation of the Christian's most important need. Not necessarily *more* prayer, but properly executed prayer. Prayer doesn't come naturally to selfish flesh. It must be learned, it must be acquired, it must be part of a disciplined life. The asking is the easy part, it's the application and consistent practice that hinders many of us. Prayer is spiritual in nature, but in order for it to accomplish God's will it must pass through human lips, using a human voice, and with a conscious human mind and understanding.

The Lord's Prayer then is not what to pray, but how to pray. It is an outline we can use to pray for an hour a day. It gives us a form we can follow so we don't lose our focus. It trains us to put things in God's priority rather than our own priority. Don't be deceived into thinking all your prayer must be spontaneous and free-wheeling. God is a God of order, and if we are to be effective in prayer, we must make the flesh and carnal mind submit to the discipline that true prayer provides.

THE FIRST TEN MINUTES

(9) *"...Our Father which art in heaven, Hallowed be thy name."*

We established in the last part that we should always come into prayer with PRAISE. The way we approach God is more important than what we have to say when we get there.

"Enter into his gates with thanksgiving, and into his courts with praise: be thankful unto him, and bless his name." —Psalm 100:4

The idea is to read or memorize the scriptures to get that concept into our conscious thought. Why? Because we're in training remember? The first thing the carnal mind thinks about is "I", "me", and "mine." (It sings, "I wanna talk about me!") The goal of the first ten minutes is to get our minds off of us and on the one we're praying to. This can be summed up in one word...

RECOGNITION

We recognize God by calling him by name and giving him praise and worship that only He deserves. And another thing, it attracts God's attention and makes him want to stick around for the rest of your prayer time...

*"But thou art holy, O thou that **inhabitest** the praises of Israel."*
—Psalm 22:3

So, get your mind right with some praise and usher in the Lord of Glory so that you can have a conversation...

THE SECOND TEN MINUTES

After **Recognition**, comes... (10) *"Thy kingdom come. Thy will be done in earth, as it is in heaven."* The second ten minutes instructs us to come into the throne room in an attitude of ...SUBMISSION

Ouch! Now it's getting tough because here again the flesh wants to take over and say, "give me." We need to not only recognize God but submit to him as well...

A document called the *Mekilta,* is an ancient manuscript which includes a commentary on the Exodus and includes a parable. It is about a man who comes to a province and says to the people, *"May I reign over you?"* The people reply, *"What good have you done for us?" "Why should we accept your reign?"* In response the man builds a wall (to protect them), brings them water & fights battles for them. Once more he asks, *"May I reign over you?"* The people reply, *"Yes, Yes!"*

God never occupies a personal space where he is not invited and you also must willingly accept his authority over every area of your life. Then submission must be the next step in our prayer time...

"Submit yourselves therefore to God, Resist the devil and he will flee from you." —James 4:7

Victory over the enemy never comes until we first submit authority and control over to God. The blueletterbible.com adds this commentary to the use of, "Submit yourselves..."

The one of the seven usages for these words that applies the best in this situation is given as... *"to yield to one's admonition or advice." It goes on to say that there is a military application for this word but the non-military definition is explained like this...*

In the non-military use, it was "a voluntary attitude of giving in, cooperating, assuming responsibility, and carrying a burden.

LET'S TAKE IT TO THE GREEK

In the original Greek from which we get most of the N.T. translations, verse 10 would be written with the verbs listed first and can be rendered as ...

"Come, kingdom of God. Be done, will of God."

This second ten minutes is not only an invitation for God to enter our thoughts and personal space but also is a transfer of power, from our human will, to his divine will.

Larry Lea, author of the book entitled *"Could You Not Tarry One Hour?"* suggests we take this time in prayer to submit four specific areas of life...

A.) Yourself - How well does your life go when you're in complete control? Isn't that what we all look forward to when we grow up? To take charge, to be our person, to make our own choices? Well God, like any good parent, probably knows more about life than you do. He's not looking for a bunch of robots, he just simply wants the best for you.

Since he's the only one who sees and knows all, shouldn't we probably run things past him? He might want us to go in a different direction, see something a different way, know some things that he knows... and we can't do that if we have our fingers wrapped around the steering wheel so tight, even He couldn't pry them loose. (We're control freaks! – I am a man we don't stop for directions!)

"Wherefore let them that suffer according to the will of God commit the keeping of their souls to him in well doing as unto a faithful Creator." —I Peter 4:19

"And the world passeth away, and the lust thereof: but he that doeth the will of God abideth forever." —I John 2:17

Each day we must consciously, out loud, with our own voice tell God, "God, I want you to be in control, I will submit to whatever you want to do with me today."

B.) Our Family – This is when you bring your family before God. Yeah you. This is where you call out your spouse by name so God will lead them and guide them as well.

Be specific. You can pray life, blessing, strength, peace, healing, wisdom, anointing (you get the idea) into your spouse's life. Don't complain about it, pray about it! Maybe the reason your spouse isn't everything they should be is because you don't take them to God in prayer. You need to pray that God's will be done in their life.

Acts 20:32 sets forth a principle that fits... "*And now, brethren, I commend you to God, and to the word of grace, which is able to build you up, and to give you an inheritance among all them which are sanctified.*"

You can't change your spouse, but submit them, commend them to God because he can change them better than you can. One of the definitions for commend is, "to intrust, commit to one's charge."

Now how about them stubborn, disobedient, disrespectful kids. Well chances are if they're like that it has nothing to do with God and everything to do with what you allowed them to get away with! But what's done is done. We can still bring our kids by name before God and submit them into God's hand. Job did it ...

*"And it was so, when the days of their (Job's kids) feasting were gone about, that Job sent and sanctified them, and rose up early in the morning, and offered burnt offerings according to their number of them all (no blanket prayers, call each out by name!), for Job said, It may be that my sons have sinned (you can't keep them from sin, but you can take their name before God in prayer), and cursed God in their hearts. Thus did Job **continually**."*

—Job 1:5

C.) Your Church – Larry Lea recommends to touch on these four specific areas when you bring your church before God.

1.) Pastor / Ministry - Call out their name and their spouses in prayer. Two scriptures that illustrate this principle…

"But Moses' hands were heavy; and they took a stone, and put it under him, and he say thereon; and Aaron and Hur stayed up his hands , the one on the one side, and the other on the other side; and his hands were steady until the going down of the sun."

—Exodus 17:12

And Paul to the church in Colossae … *"For this cause we also, since the day we heard it, do not cease to pray for you, and to desire that ye might be filled with knowledge of his will in all wisdom and spiritual understanding."* —Colossians 1:9

2.) Leadership - Speak those names who have responsibilities within the assembly. Sunday school teachers, board members, service leaders, worship leaders, youth workers, etc.

"Finally, brethren, pray for us, that the word of the Lord may have free course (spread rapidly and triumph), and be glorified, even as it is with you:" —II Thess. 3:1

3.) Faithfulness – Not just in attendance, but everything that pertains to the service of the kingdom. Sometimes we take people for granted, but everyone needs lifted up in prayer. Remember, *"…a house divided against itself, that house cannot stand."* If half of us are home and half of us are at church we are affected. Even if ONE isn't here it could allow the enemy an advantage or opportunity he might not have had otherwise.

Hebrews 10:25 … *"Not forsaking the assembling of ourselves together, as the manner of some is; but exhorting* (this word in the Greek is translated 6 times as "pray".) *one another: and so much more, as ye see the day approaching."*

4.) Harvest – We need souls! The kingdom needs souls! We need to pray for the harvest!

John 4:35b ... *"Lift up your eyes, and look on the fields; for they are white already to harvest."*

Larry Lea shares the scripture that he uses in prayer concerning the harvest...

(5) "Fear not: for I am with thee: I will bring thy seed from the east, and gather thee from the west;

(6) I will say to the north, Give up; and to the south, Keep not back: bring my sons from far, and my daughters from the ends of the earth;

(7) Even every one that is called by my name: for I have created him for my glory, I have formed him: yea, I have made him." — Isaiah 43:5-7

It's talking about praying for God to help us bring in the harvest! Pastor Lea made it a practice to read this scripture every day in prayer and his church went from 300 to 4,789 new members in 1985. In one three-month period in 1986 they saw over 500 people added to the church. He attributes that growth to praying directly to the harvest!

5.) The Nation – Yes, pray for those who govern, whether local, state or federal. Know their names, call them out in prayer. Pray God moves in them with wisdom and grace. God can do what we can't...

(1) "I exhort (pray) therefore, that, first of all supplications, prayers, intercessions, and giving of thanks, be made for all men;

(2) For kings, and for all that are in authority; that we may lead a quiet and peaceable life in all godliness and honesty. —I Timothy 2:1-2

FIRST TEN MINUTES – RECOGNITION

SECOND TEN MINUTES - SUBMISSION

Chapter 29

Violent Prayers

Matt. 11:12-14 ... (12) *"And from the days of John the Baptist until now the kingdom of heaven suffereth violence, and the violent take it by force.*

(13) For all the prophets and the law prophesied until John.

(14) And if ye will receive it, this is Elias, which was for to come.

New English Translation

"From the days of John the Baptist until now the kingdom of heaven has suffered violence, and forceful people lay hold of it."

Revised Standard Version

"From the days of John the Baptist until now the kingdom of heaven has suffered violence, and men of violence take it by force."

Amplified Bible

"And from the days of John the Baptist until the present time the kingdom of heaven has endured violent assault, and violent men seize it by force [as a precious prize] – a share in the heavenly kingdom is sought for with most ardent and intense exertion."

And another translation says, *"... and the energetic seize it."*

The time has come to put aside our Pollyanna type prayers, our lay me down to sleep prayers, our gimme, gimme, gimme, my name is Jimmy prayers, our plastic, placid, and unrepentant prayers.

If you haven't noticed the kingdom of Heaven is under attack. The violent are trying to overthrow God's kingdom, His Church, His body, and His Bride. They're not just trying to destroy America, they're trying to kill, steal, and destroy what God has established on the earth.

Yes, Matt. 10:16 says, ... *"Behold, I send you forth as sheep in the midst of wolves: be ye therefore wise as serpents, and harmless as doves."*

But it says also in Ecc. 3:1 ... *"To every thing there is <u>a season</u>, and <u>a time</u> (event of time) to every purpose under the heaven:*

Jewish Tanakh – *"A season is set for everything, a time for every experience under heaven."*

And then it gets specific for 7 more verses and finally in verse 8 it says this ...

Ecc. 3:8 ... *"A time to love, and a time to hate; <u>a time of war, and a time of peace</u>."*

The kingdom of heaven is God's government, God's system, God's people living under His rule and reign on the earth. Under His authority and anointing. And under His guidance and direction. Remember mankind has "dominion" on the Earth. We are both the physical and the spiritual gatekeepers of everything that moves, breaths, and operates on the earth.

And so according to Matthew chapter 12 this heavenly kingdom on the earth is subject to violent attacks by the enemies of God and the Church. If God had not intended for us to engage in this conflict in some-way He would not have offered us ...

The helmet of Salvation, we wouldn't need the breastplate of Righteousness, there would be no purpose in putting Truth around our waist, or preparation and peace on our feet. And He definitely wouldn't have made available a shield of Faith, and put something beyond razor sharp in our hand, the Two-edged Sword of the Spirit, if He didn't intend for us to engage the enemy in some way.

No, we do not fight flesh and blood, we don't engage this conflict with earthly weapons. In fact, we engage the enemy with spiritual weapons. And as passive as prayer would seem to our human nature, it has powerful, authoritative anointing in the spiritual dimension.

The battle is the Lord's but anything that is spiritual that affects the earth passes through the natural man. Our prayers release angels with flaming swords to fight an enemy much wiser and stronger than we. Our prayers release the justice and judgement of God. Our prayers bind the principalities of the enemy's kingdom. Our prayers bind sickness and disease. Our prayers loose the virtue and healing power of God.

So having said all that, there is then ***a time and a season*** when the church lays aside the olive branch and the dove and fights to the finish with everything they have. If there is a time and a season for the Lion and the lamb then there is a time for war and a time for peace.

This is obviously a time and a season to war. In the book of Esther, the unchangeable word of an earthly king decreed that the Jews would be subject to total destruction. So, what did they do? Sit around sucking their thumbs waiting for the sword? No! They took the fight directly to Haman through intercession to the highest authority and power. No, they could not change the decree, but they could fight and defend themselves, kill the enemy, and spoil them. No, we do not fight in the physical! The book of Esther is using a physical example of a principle of spiritual warfare.

Esther did not plunge a knife into the heart of Haman. She fasted, she prayed, she interceded to the highest physical (and spiritual) power and authority. The rest also happened (deliverance) by and through earthly agents (Mordecai).

IN TIMES OF SPIRITUAL CONFLICT ...

The Church must get a warfare mentality. We must pray and fast with a warfare mentality. We must have an Elijah attitude!

In the Bible it mentions Elijah by name for a reason and a purpose. Elijah wasn't just a prophet he was a prayer warrior. When Elijah prayed it was with passion and zeal. When Elijah prayed fire came down from heaven. (At least 3 times) When Elijah prayed the rain stopped on the earth for 3 ½ years. When Elijah prayed the dead came back to life. When Elijah prayed the waters of the river parted like the Red Sea. When Elijah prayed false prophets, kings and queens were defeated. When Elijah prayed the supernatural was seen in the natural.

The time and the season is for war. The time and the season is for passionate, powerful, anointed intercession against a spiritual enemy.

JUST TO BE FAIR AND BALANCED ... (unlike Fox News)

Some genius would say Hey! What about ...

Luke 9:51-56 ... (51) *And it came to pass, when the time was come that he should be received up, he stedfastly set his face to go to Jerusalem,*

(52) And sent messengers before his face: and they went, and entered into a village of the Samaritans, to make ready for him.

(53) And they did not receive him, because his face was as though he would go to Jerusalem.

(54) <u>And when his disciples James and John saw this, they said, Lord, wilt thou that we command fire to come down from heaven, and consume them, even as Elias did</u>?

(55) But he turned, and rebuked them, and said, Ye know not what manner of spirit ye are of.

(56) For the Son of man is not come to destroy men's lives, but to save them. And they went to another village."

Yeah, what about that!? Well, that's easy! In that time and in that season, Jesus was the Lamb of God. His overall mission is to seek and to save the lost. But it is also clearly seen that there will be a time when the Lamb of God becomes the Lion of the Tribe of Judah. The Lion comes in times of war, not the Lamb. The Lion comes with justice and judgement, not the Lamb. The Lion comes with zeal and passion, not the Lamb. The Lion comes with power and authority, not the Lamb. ... and at times so should the Church!

GOD COMES TO EARTH AS BOTH SAVIOUR & JUDGE.

Isa 34:8 ... *"For it is the day of the LORD'S vengeance, and the year of recompences for the controversy of Zion."*

Isa 35:4 ... *"Say to them that are of a fearful heart, Be strong, fear not: behold, your God will come with vengeance, even God with a recompence; he will come and save you."*

Isa 47:3 ..." ... *I will take vengeance, and I will not meet thee as a man."*

Isa 59:17 ... *"For he put on righteousness as a breastplate, and an helmet of salvation upon his head;* **and he put on the garments of vengeance for clothing,** *and was clad with zeal as a cloke."*

Isa 61:2 ... *"To proclaim the acceptable year of the LORD, and the day of vengeance of our God; to comfort all that mourn;"*

Isa 63:4 ... *"For the day of vengeance is in mine heart, and the year of my redeemed is come."*

You might say well, that's O.T. ... okay here we Go!

2 Thess. 1:6-10 ... (6) *"Seeing it is a righteous thing with God to recompense tribulation to them that trouble you;*

(7) And to you who are troubled rest with us, when the Lord Jesus shall be revealed from heaven with his mighty angels,

(8) In flaming fire taking vengeance on them that know not God, and that obey not the gospel of our Lord Jesus Christ:

(9) Who shall be punished with everlasting destruction from the presence of the Lord, and from the glory of his power;

(10) When he shall come to be glorified in his saints, and to be admired in all them that believe (because our testimony among you was believed) in that day."

IN OTHER WORD'S ...

It's time for John Wayne, not Tom Hanks. It's time for warfare, not welfare. It's time for the Lion, and the Lamb. It's time for lightning and thunder, not peaceful protests. It's time for intercession, not intermission. It's time for the fear of the Lord, not the fear of the Anti-Christ. It's time to have zeal, passion, authority and power, not apologies or compromise!

It's time for some appointed, anointed violent prayers that reach the throne of God. That release waves of angelic host of heaven with flaming swords doing great battle bringing vengeance and justice to all the enemies of God in the heavenlies and on the earth!

Chapter 30

"Welease the Seecwet Weapon!"

2 Corinthians 10:3-6

(3) "For though we walk in the flesh, we do not war after the flesh:

(4) (For the weapons of our warfare are not carnal, but mighty through God to the pulling down of strong holds;)

(5) Casting down imaginations, and every high thing that exalteth itself against the knowledge of God, and bringing into captivity every thought to the obedience of Christ;

(6) And having in a readiness to revenge all disobedience, when your obedience is fulfilled."

Ephesians 6:10-20

(10) "Finally, my brethren, be strong in the Lord, and in the *power of his might.*

(11) *Put on the whole armour of God, that ye may be able to stand against the wiles of the devil.*

(12) *For we wrestle not against flesh and blood, but against principalities, against powers, against the rulers of the darkness of this world, against spiritual wickedness in high places.*

(13) *Wherefore take unto you the whole armour of God, that ye*

may be able to withstand in the evil day, and having done all, to stand.

(14) Stand therefore, having your loins girt about with truth, and having on the breastplate of righteousness;

(15) And your feet shod with the preparation of the gospel of peace;

(16) Above all, taking the shield of faith, wherewith ye shall be able to quench all the fiery darts of the wicked.

(17) And take the helmet of salvation, and the sword of the Spirit, which is the word of God:

(18) Praying always with all prayer and supplication in the Spirit, and watching thereunto with all perseverance and supplication for all saints;

(19) And for me, that utterance may be given unto me, that I may open my mouth boldly, to make known the mystery of the gospel,

(20) For which I am an ambassador in bonds: that therein I may speak boldly, as I ought to speak."

"WELEASE THE SEECWET WEAPON!"

That line was from a 1986 animated film by Stephen Spielberg called An American Tail, where the mice create a weapon to fight against their enemy the cats.

But with maybe a little less humor, and more of the scripture, the church in this hour must understand these things ...

We are in a life and death struggle with an enemy who we can't see, touch, or fight with conventional methods.

God has equipped us with protection in this conflict with the whole armor of God.

But He has also given us a secret weapon to fight, defeat, and conquer, any enemy we face in this world!

The enemy has little or no defense against it and it will ensure complete victory!

So ... I thought I would be a real smart guy and look up "secret weapon" on the internet. Here's a sample of what I found ...

Secret Weapon Unleashed In Baghdad
By Bill Dash, c. 2003

A nightmarish US super weapon reportedly was employed by American ground forces during chaotic street fighting in Baghdad. The secret tank-mounted weapon was witnessed in all its frightening power by Majid al-Ghazali, a seasoned Iraqi infantryman who described the device and its gruesome effects as unlike anything he had ever encountered in his lengthy military service. The disturbing revelation is yet another piece of cinematic evidence brought back from postwar Iraq by intrepid filmmaker Patrick Dillon.

In the film, al-Ghazali, whose English is less than fluent, describes the weapon as reminiscent of a flame-thrower, only immensely more powerful. It is unclear what principle the weapon is based on.

Searching for a description, al-Ghazali said it appeared to be shooting concentrated lightning bolts rather than just ordinary flames. Drawing on his many years as a professional engineer, al-Ghazali speculates that radiation of some kind probably figures into the weapon's hideous capabilities. Like all men in Saddam's Iraq, al-Ghazali was compelled to serve in the Iraqi equivalent of the Army National Guard and fought in three wars over the past thirty-odd years. Via email, he told me he has seen virtually every type of conventional weapon employed in battle, and is well acquainted with their effects on people and machines, but nothing in his extensive combat experience prepared him for the shock of what he saw in Baghdad on April 12th.

On that date, al-Ghazali and his family sheltered in their house as a fierce street battle erupted in his neighborhood. In the midst of the fighting, he noticed that the Americans had called up an oddly configured tank. Then to his amazement the tank suddenly let loose a blinding stream of what seemed like fire and lightning, engulfing a large passenger bus and three automobiles. Within seconds the bus had become semi-molten, sagging "like a wet rag" as he put it. He said the bus rapidly melted under this withering blast, shrinking until it was a twisted blob about the dimensions of a VW bug. As if that were not bizarre enough, al-Ghazali explicitly describes seeing numerous human bodies shriveled to the size of newborn babies. By the time local street fighting ended that day, he estimates between 500 and 600 soldiers and civilians had been cooked alive as a result of the mysterious tank-mounted device.

Then in one of the concluding paragraphs the filmmaker says this in conclusion ...

"I've seen a smorgasbord of destruction in my life," he said, "flame-throwers, napalm, white phosphorous, thermite, you name it. I know of nothing short of an H-bomb that conceivably might cause a bus to instantly liquefy or that can flash-broil a human body down to the size of an infant. God pity humanity if that thing is a preview of what's in store for the 21st century."

IF THAT WEREN'T ENOUGH ...

There is also an article about what the U.S. military calls the Objective Individual Combat Weapon.

In the article it states this about this weapon ...

The OICW is the next generation weapon. The ammo actually has a computer on-board. You thought smart bombs were cool. Well, this gun takes smart weapons to the next level. Imagine being in a sniper fight with your enemy. Both your enemy and you are hiding behind heavy bullet proof shelters, But you have the advantage. You have a OICW. Your weapon has a built -in range finder. Now that you know the distance between you and your enemy, for example 720 feet away. You don't need to directly hit him if he is hiding behind something. You point your gun over his position or behind him. The gun actually programs the ammo to explode at 725 feet which will blast shrapnel all over. With the OICW, line of sight is no longer a rule for sniper fights.

Now here's the thing folks. **If it's on the internet, it's not a secret anymore!** But even then, it doesn't make those weapons any less effective!

GOD'S SECRET WEAPON FOR THE CHURCH ...

In Ephesians 6 Paul gives the church vital intelligence about our conflict with our enemy. He provides insight and instruction about this spiritual conflict listing all the things God has provided for us if we choose to use them.

He tells us to put on the whole armor of God, ...

Which includes ... *the Helmet of Salvation, the Breastplate of Righteousness, a belt of Truth, the Shield of Faith, and the proper foot gear of the Gospel.*

BUT ARMOR ISN'T WHAT I WOULD CALL A WEAPON.

It's not till vs. 17 that Paul describes what I would call an actual weapon, the Sword of the Spirit, which is the word of God (Hebrews 4:12), but then Paul actually tells us what this secret weapon is for the Church of the Living God.

Ephesians 6:18 ... **<u>"Praying always with all prayer and</u> <u>supplication in the Spirit</u>**, *and watching thereunto with all perseverance and supplication for all saints;"*

And you're saying, WHAAAAAAATTTTT? ***Prayer is our secret weapon?*** Are you serious?

But let's look at the scripture both O.T. and N.T.

In Genesis 20:17 Abraham was in a bad situation with King Abimilech ... But it says, ***So Abraham prayed unto God***, ...

In I Samuel 1:10 when Hannah wanted a baby and couldn't, it says, ...

"And she was in bitterness of soul, ***and prayed unto the LORD****, and wept sore."*

1 Sam. 2:1 ... *"****And Hannah prayed****, and said, My heart rejoiceth in the LORD, mine horn is exalted in the LORD:* ***my mouth is enlarged over mine enemies; because I rejoice in thy salvation.****"*

In II Kings 4:32-35 Elisha was faced with death...

(32) "And when Elisha was come into the house, behold, the child was dead, and laid upon his bed.

(33) He went in therefore, and shut the door upon them twain, ***and prayed unto the LORD.***

(34) And he went up, and lay upon the child, and put his mouth upon his mouth, and his eyes upon his eyes, and his hands upon his hands: and he stretched himself upon the child; and the flesh of the child waxed warm.

(35) Then he returned, and walked in the house to and fro; and

went up, and stretched himself upon him: and the child sneezed seven times, and the child opened his eyes."

And in again Elisha is faced with being surrounded by the enemy ...

II Kings 6:16-18 ...

(16) "And he answered, Fear not: for they that be with us are more than they that be with them.

(17) **And Elisha prayed,** *and said, LORD, I pray thee, open his eyes, that he may see. And the LORD opened the eyes of the young man; and he saw: and, behold, the mountain was full of horses and chariots of fire round about Elisha.*

(18) And when they came down to him, **Elisha prayed unto the LORD,** *and said, Smite this people, I pray thee, with blindness. And he smote them with blindness according to the word of Elisha."*

It says Job prayed for his friends and his captivity ended...

Daniel prayed when the king's decree went forth, it didn't keep him from the Lion's den but it was God's secret weapon.

It says Jonah prayed in the belly of a fish and God heard him...

Matt. 26:42-44 Jesus was in the garden and in the middle of great conflict, but he released the secret weapon ....

The disciples in Acts 4:31 when they were faced with opposition from the authorities it says, **"And when they had prayed,** *the place was shaken where they were assembled together; and they were all filled with the Holy Ghost, and they spake the word of God with boldness."*

And when Paul and Silas were put in prison Acts 16:25 and their chains fell off, and the doors opened and they were delivered simply because... *"... at midnight prayed and sang praises unto God."*

And in Acts 28:8 when a man needed healing from a serious disease *Paul prayed and God healed him...*

WE NEED TO *"RELEASE THE SECRET WEAPON!"*

You want to know why prayer is still a secret weapon? It's not a secret to the enemy because it is clearly the most effective weapon ever created and the enemy knows how powerful and effective prayer is. And they also hope the Church never realizes how powerful it is.

In other words, it's not a secret to the enemy, but if it's a secret, it's only a secret to us, the church!

Again, we need to Release the Secret Weapon!

Chapter 31

"The Lord's Prayer"

Part IV

Matthew 6:9-13 / Luke 11:2-4

(9) "After this manner therefore pray ye: Our Father which art in heaven, Hallowed be thy name.

(10) Thy kingdom come. Thy will be done in earth as it is in heaven.

(11) Give us this day our daily bread.

(12) And forgive us our debts, as we forgive our debtors.

(13) And lead us not into temptation, but deliverance from evil: for thine is the kingdom, and the power, and the glory, for ever. Amen."

INTRODUCTION

The Lord's Prayer is not something just to be quoted. It is an outline, a model prayer wherein we can train ourselves to pray in six separate areas of life. We should make it our goal to designate a time and a place and devote them to the sole purpose of communing with God.

Jesus in a previous scripture before he delivered to his disciples the Lord's Prayer gave them a very important principle of an effective and powerful prayer life.

"But thou, when thou prayest, enter into thy closet, and when thou hast shut thy door, pray to thy Father which is in secret; (My

word: private) ... *and thy Father which seeth in secret shall reward thee openly."* —Matthew 6:6

Does Jesus mean we need to literally close ourselves off in a closet somewhere? Well, my question would be, *How important is your prayer time with God?* Yes, there are times we pray together with family and the saints. But you will not find what you need in prayer if you're answering your phone, watching the news, listening to someone complain about the government, etc. In order to shut out all the distractions, you must find an isolated spot with just you and God. Jesus provided us with an example to follow...

Matthew 14: 23... *"And when he had sent the multitude away, he went up into a mountain apart to pray: and when the evening was come, he was alone."*

It really doesn't matter if it's in the morning, the evening, or straight up high noon, the principle is this. Find a regular, isolated, private place to pour out your heart to God! Why did Jesus go to the mountain to pray? I believe it was a twofold purpose. One, the total absence of distractions and secondly, people are basically lazy. Who's going to follow Jesus UP the mountain to pray? Come on some of us wouldn't make that kind of an effort in prayer unless they were giving out free Big Macs at McDonalds. So, find a place where it's just you and God. Guard that time carefully and if life gets in the way, be determined to MAKE TIME for the most important part of any day!

THE THIRD TEN MINUTES

If our goal is to pray for one hour, then the first 10 minutes should be spent in praise to His name... this is what we'll call **recognition**. The second 10 minutes should be getting our flesh to behave and cooperate with the Spirit and we'll call that **submission**. Now we enter into our third segment of our prayer time in Matthew 6:11...

"Give us this day our daily bread."

After praise and after submitting ourselves, we will enter into a time of ***petition***. God wants to hear about our needs, just not before we recognize his sovereignty. There's nothing wrong with asking God for "things" but we need to ask at the right time and in the right way.

Now a **petition** according to the Random House College Dictionary can mean...

> 1.) *A formal request, often bearing the name of a person or body of persons in authority, soliciting some favor, right, or other benefit.*
>
> 2.) *A request, especially a respectful or humble one; a supplication or prayer: a petition for aid."*

Here again Jesus illustrates God's willingness to hear our petitions. In Matthew 6:8 Jesus is giving them (disciples) a mini seminar on prayer...

"Be not therefore like unto them: (the Pharisees / hypocrites – an actor, stage player, pretender) *for your Father knoweth what things ye have need of, before ye ask him."*

Matthew 7:7-8... *Ask, and it shall be given you; seek, and ye shall find; knock, and the door shall be opened unto you:*

(8) For everyone that asketh recieveth; and he that seeketh findeth; and to him that knocketh it shall be opened."

Now let's not get ridiculous. God is not giving us a blank check to fill in the amount. We're still being **submissive** to HIS will remember and just because you ask, he's not going to say with a giggle, *"Oh, yes I'll get that for you right away!"* But God provides us a time where we can ask him for anything. Yeah, we may not get it right away, or in the shape and color we asked for, but God invites us to ask. After all James (4:2) tells the church in his letter...

*"Ye lust, and have not: ye kill and desire to have, and cannot obtain: ye fight and war, yet ye have not, **because ye ask not**".* But

then James also makes it clear we aren't always going to get what we ask for ...

(3) *"Ye ask, and receive not, **because ye ask amiss**, ...* and from the Amplified Bible we'll finish his statement... *"your intention is, [when you get what you desire] to spend it in sensual pleasures."* (governed by breath, physical appetite and passion)

Maybe a little selfish desire, huh? God understands and sometimes He doesn't give us what we ask, because he sees and knows our true motive behind the request. But hey, at least he gave you the opportunity to ask and somewhere down the road when the "me" drops off the request and more of the "He" is added he might just say, yes.

IT'S "DAILY" BREAD!

This is illustrated in living color in the O.T. with God's kids are in the wilderness. Probably around a million of them with their babies, toddlers, and teenagers. They've got to eat right? They were totally dependent on God for their *daily* bread.

Exodus 16:2-4, 8, 14-15... *(2) And the whole congregation of the children of Israel murmured against Moses and Aaron in the wilderness:*

(3) And the children of Israel said unto them, Would to God we had died by the hand of the Lord in the land of Egypt, when we sat by the flesh pots, and when we did eat bread to the full; for ye have brought us forth into this wilderness, to kill this whole assembly with hunger.

(4) Then said the Lord unto Moses, Behold, I will rain bread from heaven for you; and the people shall go out and gather a certain rate every day, that I may prove them, whether they will walk in my law, or no.

(8) "And Moses said, This shall be, when the Lord shall give you in the evening flesh to eat, and in the morning bread to the full; for that the lord heareth your murmurings which ye murmur against

him: and what are we? Your murmurings are not against us, but against the Lord."

(14) "And when the dew that lay was gone up, behold, upon the face of the wilderness there lat a small round thing, as small as the hoar frost on the ground.

(15) And when the children of Israel saw it, they said one to another, It is manna: for they wist not what it was. And Moses said unto them, This is the bread which the Lord hath given you to eat."

You might be saying to yourself, *"What does that have to do with prayer?"* Well, we're trying to get some principles that we can get a hold of. The scripture firmly presents the idea that God is concerned with both our spiritual needs (through our pray time) and our physical needs. And both these areas need to be established and maintained on a daily basis. How long would yesterday's lunch carry us? On a normal day we think we are going to starve if we don't get three squares a day (and some snacks in between?). Well, that's the way we are designed in the natural, so why would the spiritual be any different? It's a ***daily thing***! If what in the natural wears off after a few hours (24) than maybe prayer needs to provide a daily time of spiritual provision. Prayer is the means where we talk to Him about body and soul. Yesterday's prayer only carried us as far as yesterday. We need today's prayer for today. And we'll need tomorrow's prayer for tomorrow, if there is a tomorrow. ***It's a daily thing!***

Exodus 16:20-21 ... *"Notwithstanding they hearkened not unto Moses; but some of them left of it until morning, and it bred worms, and stank: and Moses was wroth with them.*

*(21) And they gathered it every morning, every man according to his eating: and when the sun waxed hot, **it melted**."*

God probably knows our wants, needs, situations and desires before we even form the words. But it is in the daily activity of prayer where we start to understand God's ways and methods. He does care about everything we have need of. Not totally unlike

God's people gathering the manna on a daily basis, God would like us to bring our daily needs to Him in prayer!

BE SPECIFIC!

In a previous church we attended, there was a group of us men talking with our Pastor. And one of the guys mentioned that he was out of work and needed a job. The Pastor spoke up and said something like, *"What kind of job do you want?"* I don't remember the answer but he told him and then he asked him, *"Well, how much would you like to make an hour?"* Again, I can't recall the response, but I can remember that we prayed specifically for him to get the kind of job he wanted and at the hourly wage he was looking for. It must have been a couple days later and the Pastor told me that that same guy called him and told him that he not only had a job but at the exact wages that he had prayed for! It's not magic, it's not voodoo, it's not just coincidence, its being specific with a God who knows how many hairs are on your head!

Jesus puts it this way.... (11) *"If a son shall ask bread of any of you that is a father, will he give him a stone? Or if he ask a fish, will he for a fish give him a serpent?*

(12) Or if he shall ask for an egg, will he offer him a scorpion?

(13) If ye then, being evil, know how to give good gifts unto your children: how much more shall your heavenly Father give the Holy Spirit to them that ask him?" —Matt. 7:11-13

Your words have power. Use them to communicate what you need to God. Be specific. Be persistent. In Luke 11:5-8 Jesus tells a parable about a guy who needed some bread. Not yesterday, not tomorrow, but today! It was late, his friend was in bed and he made his request vocally and specifically...

(5b) *"Friend, lend me three loaves."*

And of course, the excuses fly but in verse 8 it says that he really needed that bread, so it says he became persistent in his petition to his friend...

(7) *"Though he will not rise and give him, because he is a friend,* **yet because of his importunity** *he will rise and give him as many as he needeth."*

Now that word *importunity* from several sources amounts to this. **A shameless, persistent solicitation**. We need to be specific and persistent in some of our petitions to God. Here it comes the million-dollar question... *What if God doesn't answer my prayer?* Well, I can't speak for God in every matter and request but here is an attempt.

Remember them folks in the wilderness in Exodus 16? And they were all whining about not having enough to eat? And in verse 4 God tells Mo that he's going to make it rain bread (and quail) on them. But it also said, *"... and the people shall go out and gather a certain rate every day, ...* God provided, but they had to do their part. And he also says, ... *"that I may prove* (test) *them, whether they will walk in my law or no."* Yep, it may not be a test of the emergency broadcast system, but it's only a test. The funny thing about people is we're never satisfied. God gives us what we want and need and then after a while we go, What manna again? *We had manna for the last blah, blah, blah!* It's a TEST people! Will you be obedient if God doesn't give you what you want, when you want it, and how you want it? He might simply be testing your importunity. He might be testing your spirit and your attitude. No matter what God's motive or method we must be consistent, faithful, specific, and persistent in our daily petitions.

Psalm 2:8... *"Ask of me, and I shall give thee the heathen for thine inheritance, and the uttermost part of the earth for thy possession."*

FIRST TEN MINUTES – RECOGNITION

SECOND TEN MINUTES – SUBMISSION

THIRD TEN MINUTES - PETITION

Chapter 32

He's Still Praying

John 17:9-26 ... NKJV (9) *"I pray for them. I do not pray for the world but for those whom You have given Me, for they are Yours.*

(10) "And all Mine are Yours, and Yours are Mine, and I am glorified in them.

(11) "Now I am no longer in the world, but these are in the world, and I come to You. Holy Father, keep through Your name those whom You have given Me, that they may be one as We are.

(12) "While I was with them in the world, I kept them in Your name. Those whom You gave Me I have kept; and none of them is lost except the son of perdition, that the Scripture might be fulfilled.

(13) "But now I come to You, and these things I speak in the world, that they may have My joy fulfilled in themselves.

(14) "I have given them Your word; and the world has hated them because they are not of the world, just as I am not of the world.

(15) "I do not pray that You should take them out of the world, but that You should keep them from the evil one.

(16) "They are not of the world, just as I am not of the world.

(17) "Sanctify them by Your truth. Your word is truth.

(18) As You sent Me into the world, I also have sent them into the world.

(19) "And for their sakes I sanctify Myself, that they also may be sanctified by the truth.

(20) "I do not pray for these alone, but also for those who will believe in Me through their word;

(21) "that they all may be one, as You, Father, are in Me, and I in You; that they also may be one in Us, that the world may believe that You sent Me.

(22) "And the glory which You gave Me I have given them, that they may be one just as We are one:

(23) "I in them, and You in Me; that they may be made perfect in one, and that the world may know that You have sent Me, and have loved them as You have loved Me.

(24) "Father, I desire that they also whom You gave Me may be with Me where I am, that they may behold My glory which You have given Me; for You loved Me before the foundation of the world.

(25) "O righteous Father! The world has not known You, but I have known You; and these have known that You sent Me.

(26) "And I have declared to them Your name, and will declare it, that the love with which You loved Me may be in them, and I in them."

To say the least, prayer is what empowers men and women with the power, authority and relationship of God. Prayer is what connects the human with the divine. Prayer is the temporal touching the eternal. And we have lost much understanding of prayer.

PRAYER HABITS OF FAMOUS MEN ...

James Duncan, preaching with great unction and power, was asked what was the secret of such powerful preaching. "The secret," he said, was "thirteen hours of consecutive prayer."

When asked the secret of his spiritual power, Charles Spurgeon said: "Knee work! Knee work!"

Livingston of Shotts, on two different occasions, preached with such power that in each service 500 were converted. Both sermons were preceded by a night of prayer.

Charles Finney, after spending a day in the woods in prayer and fasting, preached that night in a phenomenally irreligious congregation. The sermon was accompanied by such divine power that the whole congregation, except one man, fell prostrate upon the floor, and voiced their agony under conviction of sin, in such loud outcries that the preacher was forced to stop.

Of "Uncle" John Vassar, The Tract Society colporteur, his pastor says: "He absolutely prayed day and night—prayed about everything, prayed for almost everything, prayed with almost everybody he met.

"He prayed when he went out and when he came in. He prayed before every religious service, and then prayed all the way through it. I have occupied the same room with him night after night, and rarely went to sleep without hearing him in prayer, or awoke without finding him in prayer."

But what I want to focus on is that Jesus not only taught the disciples how to pray, but He practiced prayer Himself throughout His earthly ministry. There seems much debate about how many prayers Jesus prayed.

The folks at *Quotes* say that there are 38 prayers of Jesus listed in the Gospels. At JesusAlive.cc and *lifecoach4god.life* they say that Jesus prayed 25 prayers. www.faithgateway.com counts at least ten. And on *Answers.com* the "best" answer says this, *Jesus* prayed, of course, yet his recorded prayer (his actual words prayed) are relatively few. There are at least 5, possibly 6.

Without taking up much time and space here is a representation of the spoken prayers of the man Christ Jesus...

Matt. 11:25 ... (25) *"At that time Jesus answered and said, I thank thee, O Father, Lord of heaven and earth, because thou hast hid these things from the wise and prudent, and hast revealed them unto babes.*

(26) Even so, Father: for so it seemed good in thy sight."

Matt. 26:39 & 42 ... *(39) "And he went a little further, and fell on his face, and prayed, saying, O my Father, if it be possible, let this cup pass from me: nevertheless not as I will, but as thou wilt."*

(42) "He went away again the second time, and prayed, saying, O my Father, if this cup may not pass away from me, except I drink it, thy will be done."

Luke 23:46 ... *"And when Jesus had cried with a loud voice, he said, Father, into thy hands I commend my spirit: and having said thus, he gave up the ghost."*

But no matter the actual recorded number there is without a doubt sufficient evidence that Jesus did more than teach about prayer He emphatically, faithfully, and powerfully practiced prayer.

THE GREATEST PRAYER WARRIOR
...THE MAN CHRIST JESUS!

His ministry wasn't just about doing miracles, it wasn't just about showing us a human example, it wasn't just about dying on the cross and rising from the dead on the third day. EVERYTHING that Jesus did in the flesh was only possible through His times of prayer.

- Jesus prayed because he was a man in every way.
- Jesus prayed because it connected His flesh with the Spirit of God.
- Jesus prayed because in order for His flesh to accomplish the will of God, prayer provided the power to do the impossible.

Heb. 7:25 ... KJV *"Wherefore he is able also to save them to the uttermost that come unto God by him, seeing he ever liveth to make intercession for them."*

The Amplified Bible ... Therefore He is able to save forever (completely, perfectly, for eternity) those who come to God through Him, since He always lives to intercede and intervene on their behalf [with God.]"

BUT HERE'S THE THING...

Just because He has ascended into heaven, He's not just hanging around waiting for the clock to run out! He's not watching TV LAND reruns, He's not filing His nails, taking naps, or curled up reading a good book!

You know what He's doing right now? He's STILL PRAYING! The writer of Hebrews pulls back the curtain of the spiritual dimension where Jesus "ever liveth" to intercede for us! The Amplified Bible uses the word "always."

AND THAT'S WHY ...

You're never alone when you fall, you're never alone when you fail, you're never alone in the valley or on the mountain top, because He's STILL PRAYING!

Chapter 33

Hindered Prayers

1 Pet. 3:7 ... *"Likewise, ye husbands, dwell with them according to knowledge, giving honour unto the wife, as unto the weaker vessel, and as being heirs together of the grace of life; <u>that your prayers be not hindered</u>."*

Other than God Himself and His Word there is nothing on earth which touches heaven more powerful than prayer. Prayer is the power of the Christian life. Prayer is the weapon that sets the enemy to flight. Prayer is the compelling force behind the love which constrains us and forges the bond of peace and unity in the body of Christ.

If prayer is anything, then it is everything. Without prayer we are lost. Without prayer we are sick and afflicted. Without prayer we are cursed with the unclean, carnal and demonic. Without it we are without hope, peace, love, and joy. Without prayer we are defeated. Without prayer we are divided. And without prayer we are dead, both physically and spiritually.

And so, it stands to reason that besides fearing God and His Word, Satan fears the effectual fervent prayer of all the saints of God. He knows his end, but that does not stop him from waging warfare against us. If we determine in our hearts to pray, Satan himself does not have the power to stop you. But he does have strategies and devices to "hinder" your prayers. To make them less effective than or less powerful so that he can recover more quickly from the blows when they land.

The praying saint of God and the praying Church must be aware of all of Satan's devices but especially at this particular hour when prayer is so crucial and vital to release the presence and the power of God. If Satan cannot stop your prayers altogether through neglect or distractions than he will certainly try to "hinder" your prayers.

WORD STUDIES ARE COOL ...

When studying the Word of God, we must be aware of at least two things. The literal meaning of the Word, because God does not waste words on metaphors or just symbolic meanings. And the law or principle behind the Word. The effectiveness and the authority of the Word of God lies not just in its absolute meaning but in its endurance and application in its principles to every culture and generation.

So, let's focus on the last six words of I Peter 3:7 ...

KJV ... "that your prayers be not hindered."

NIV ... "so that nothing will hinder your prayers."

AMPLIFIFIED ... "in order that your prayers may not be hindered and cut off. – Otherwise you cannot pray effectively."

Sometimes to our modern western minds we do not always comprehend the significance or the weight behind certain words that the apostles and New Testament writers used. Whether somehow lost in translation or we are too lazy to study it out for ourselves doesn't really matter if we fail to apply the proper meaning.

In the King James version of I Pet. 3:7 the word "hindered" means the following according to Strong's Con.

The original Greek word (Strong's -G1581) *ekkopto* which is a verb derived from two Greek words which means ...

To cut out, cut off and includes exscind, to frustrate.

So, if I were to evaluate that definition, I would say that the meaning includes both a passive meaning (frustrated) and the more aggressive meaning (to cut off) But both Strong's and Thayer's Greek Lexicon give the example of a tree hew down or the branch of a tree cut off.

I guess what I'm trying to say is, "A tree with a branch cut off, may not kill it but it's severe injury can hinder it from producing its full potential. The only way to truly kill a tree is to kill the roots.

Yeah, I know that sometimes pruning is necessary, but that's for God to decide. My point is this, Satan may not be able to kill your prayer or your prayer life, simply because he doesn't have that kind of power or authority. But he can and will hinder you either through human relationships or direct demonic interference.

Luke 11:52 ... *"Woe unto you, lawyers! for ye have taken away the key of knowledge: ye entered not in yourselves, and them that were entering in ye hindered." (G2967)*

Rom 15:22 ... *"For which cause also I have been much <u>hindered</u> (G1465) from coming to you."*

1 Thess. 2:18 ... *"Wherefore we would have come unto you, even I Paul, once and again; but Satan <u>hindered</u> us." (G1465)*

The subject of those three scriptures isn't necessarily about prayer but they carry with them the consistent principle about being hindered. Two of those scriptures are from Paul's letter to the Church and is different from Peter's Greek word for "hindered" but it is also a verb and means to cut off as well.

Luke's word for hindered may be a verb as well but indicates a more passive application. It includes these definitions ... *to hinder, prevent, forbid, withhold, deny, refuse, keep from, withstand. (oppose)*

SO, IF YOUR PRAYERS SEEM TO BE POWERLESS ...

It could be either the enemy is directly attacking you from the spiritual dimension or there are human conditions, conflicts, or curses that are hindering the power and effectiveness of your prayers. The Holy Ghost along with the Word of God has the ability to help us discern for ourselves what that may be. But as long as it remains, your prayers will be hindered.

So, pray for discernment. Pray that your hindrance is REVEALED in detail. When that has been revealed then take authority in the name of Jesus Christ for that hindrance to be REMOVED.

Satan make not be able to keep you from praying, or kill your prayers but he knows how to use both the human and the spiritual to hinder you.

A PRAYER FOR YOUR PRAYERS ...

From a website called "Knowing Jesus" ...

A Prayer to Remove Hindrances To Fruitfulness

Heavenly Father, I pray that You would remove any areas in my life that hinder me from being fruitful in Your service. Thank You, that You have given me everything that is needful for godly living and a fruitful life.

I praise and thank You for the engrafted divine nature that I received when I was born from above, which enables me to escape the corruption of this world system and empowers me to overcome the desires of the flesh.

Deliver me from the many daily temptations and keep me I pray, from being swayed by the deceit of the enemy who masquerades as an angel-of-light, and yet is a roaring lion, seeking whom he may devour.

Search my heart for any hidden sin that may hinder my spiritual growth, and discover in me any areas that need to be cut away at the root, which are preventing me from living a truly fruitful life. And I pray that You would finish the good work that You started in me, so that I may be fruitful in Your service, to Your praise and glory. This I ask in Jesus' name,

Amen.

Source: https://prayer.knowing-jesus.com/prayer/a-prayer-to-remove-hindrances-to-fruitfulness-1561

Chapter 34

"The Lord's Prayer"

Part V

Matthew 6:9-13 / Luke 11:2-4

(9) "After this manner therefore pray ye: Our Father which art in heaven, Hallowed be thy name.

(10) Thy kingdom come. Thy will be done in earth as it is in heaven.

(11) Give us this day our daily bread.

(12) And forgive us our debts, as we forgive our debtors.

(13) And lead us not into temptation, but deliver us from evil: for thine is the kingdom, and the power, and the glory, for ever. Amen."

INTRODUCTION

You might be trying to pray for an hour. How's that working for you? If you're like many of us, probably not so good. I believe this generation has been spoiled to the point where we think we don't have to pray like they used too. I think technology and modern conveniences have robbed us of the need for a "hands on" approach. You see I believe that prayer stands alone as the one thing we can't computerize, digitize, or modernize. It is our generation's thinking that we can take something like prayer and make it more convenient. We've been deceived into thinking that prayer is outdated, archaic, and old fashioned and if it is such, not worth the effort. (How about E-Prayers? Something to save time and energy. I don't think there's an App for that.)

But some things still require us to get down on our knees, put our face to the floor, and cry out to God. In God's kingdom there is no alternative, there is no substitute, there is no new technology. Prayer is nothing but putting ourselves under the authority of a sovereign God.

And there is no way to find an easier more convenient way. No short cuts, no substitutes, no kidding!

"I have been driven many times upon my knees by the overwhelming conviction that I had nowhere else to go. My own wisdom and that of all about me seemed insufficient for that day."
—Abraham Lincoln

We tend to use prayer as a last resort, but God wants it to be our first line of defense. We pray when there's nothing else we can do, but God wants us to pray before we do anything at all.

Most of us would prefer, however, to spend our time doing something that will get immediate results. We don't want to wait for God to resolve matters in his good time because his idea of 'good time' is seldom in sync with ours." —Oswald Chambers

"He who kneels the most, stands the best." - D. L. Moody

"No man is greater than his prayer life. The Pastor who is not praying is playing; the people who are not praying are straying. We have many organizers but few agonizers; many players and payers, few pray-ers; many singers, few clingers; lots of pastors, few wrestlers; many fears, few tears; much fashion, little passion; many interferers, few intercessors; many writers, but few fighters. Failing here, (prayer) we fail everywhere." - Leonard Ravenhill

Prayer is a discipline, our training, our telling the flesh we're going to mind the Spirit for a change. If revival is our endgame, then prayer must be the driving force. Nothing else will get us to where we need to be. Let's see if we can follow the formula.

THE FOURTH TEN MINUTES

So far, we have a model given to the disciples (and us) that will help us pray for one hour. Six ten-minute segments where we pray like God wants us to pray. (You mean I can't even pray the way I want to pray?) Well, if you want to be effective and powerful in your prayer life, then Yeah!

So far, we have started with **recognition**, then taken the time to be in **submission**, after that we took all of our **petitions** to God properly, and now we are ready for verse 12...

"And forgive us our debts, as we forgive our debtors."

Before we get into its application let's look a little at the background of the writer of this statement and its meaning. Before he was one of the disciples of Jesus, the Bible records that Matthew was a tax collector. And so right off we can see why he chose to use the words debt and debtors. He took the concept of prayer and put it terms he was familiar with. And not just him, but aren't we all too familiar with debt. (Enough said.) Well, let's just cut to the chase. What Matthew was referring to in his own way was the concept of (OUR SIN) and people who OFFEND us. Right? If you haven't figured it out by now let me explain. Just because you have been through the salvation process you still deal with your sinful flesh, desires, thoughts, actions, etc. every day. And unless you live in a cave by yourself you will encounter what I like to call... People. And people have a funny way about them that can offend us from time to time. Yep, you're just never going to get away from either of those things.

Which brings these issues to God at the proper time in CONFESSION...

John in his first epistle to the church says... *"If we confess our sins, he is faithful and just to forgive us our sins, and to cleanse us from all unrighteousness."* —I John 1:9

And then Mark gives us the second part of that equation... *"And when ye stand praying, forgive, if ye have ought against any: that your Father also which is in heaven may forgive you your trespasses."*

(26) But if ye do not forgive, neither will your Father which is in heaven forgive your trespasses." —Mark 11:25-26

Before we go any further, we must clarify the words debt and debtor. In the world of finance there is a saying that whoever has the gold has the power. When it comes to debt and money whoever you owe money to in some way owns you or at the very least has a measure of power and influence over you. You are indebted to that institution. So at least in the Apostle Matthew's mind, sin and offenses were similar in their dynamic.

When we sin, and odds are we will, we will be under somebody's power because of that sin. Either our enemy the devil or God through the person of Jesus Christ. Unrepented sin places us under the devil's direct control and influence. But when we repent of those sins, although we are delivered by the blood of Jesus, we are then under the power and protection of God. It's a matter of choosing who you are going to relinquish control too. Many times, it's just a matter of **letting go**.

We're not getting into that Disney "Frozen" thing!

There's an old story about a child who snuck into his mother's kitchen while she wasn't there, simply to get a cookie. He looked down in the jar and saw that it was filled with delicious cookies. Rather than take just one he grabbed a hand full and when he tried to pull his hand out it got stuck from too many cookies in his hand. Right then his mother walked in and quickly saw what was taking place. She stopped and said two words to her young son. *"Let go."* When he realized that he would never be able to get his hand out otherwise he released the cookies and was free of the cookie jar.

Now what does that have to do with debt and sin? Those cookies represent the things we hold on to. Yep, believe it or not we will hold on to some things and that puts it in control of the cookie jar. Indulge me here. The devil or our enemy is the cookie jar. As long as we hold on to the "cookies" we are under the direct influence of that cookie jar. It may not control us but it will hinder everything we will try to do in life. What's the answer? "Let it go!"

Paul said it this way to the church... *"Brethren, I count not myself to have apprehended: but this one thing I do, forgetting those things which are behind, and reaching forth unto those things which are before,*

(14) I press toward the mark for the prize of the high calling of God in Christ Jesus." —Philippians 3:13-14

If Paul were alive today, he would probably say it something like this. *"Let it go, man!" In order to go forward you can't hold on to what's behind you!"*

THE DUAL NATURE OF FORGIVENESS

In this portion of the Lord's Prayer we clearly see that there are two distinct parts to our praying. There is a receiving and a giving. There is man receiving forgiveness from God for our debts (sins) and man giving other men (and women) forgiveness for their offences (sins). Jesus made it clear that we would be faced with that second part.

Matthew 18:7 ... *"Woe unto the world because of offences! For it must needs be that offences come; but woe to that man by whom the offence cometh!"*

The Amplified Bible puts the second half of that scripture as... *It is necessary that temptations come, but woe to the person on whose account or by whom the temptation comes.*

Now it's going to get a little more interesting. The original Greek work for "offence" literally means to trap or snare. Another definition includes these, ... *to entrap, entice to sin, make to offend.* What does that mean? Well, if we're not willing to let go of those "offences" then it can not only be a snare or trap to you, but you also are activating the release of the one who offended you. If you don't let go, they in essence have a certain measure of power over you. They become a *debtor.* Lets' look at Matt. 6:12 one more time...

"And forgive us our debts, as we forgive our debtors."

According to blueletterbible.com the word *"forgive"* (G863 Strong's) has three possible meanings or applications. The first one literally leaped off the computer screen when it said, *to let go, let alone, let be.* And the word *"debtors"* (plural) has two definitions the one we will use here says, *one who has yet made amends to whom he has injured."* So based on those two examples what we are doing in the fourth ten minutes is letting God take our sins (and their effects) from us and if we can use blueletterbible. com to paraphrase the second half...

"...as we let go of the one who has yet made amends to whom he has injured."

I think I just heard a loud explosion! So evidently forgiveness is more than saying "sorry" or being "sorry." It is releasing that which has you snared or entrapped! Let it Go! Release it! Get rid of it! Delete your cookies! Wipe the record clean!

LET'S GET REAL

In this ten-minute segment we need to accomplish two things. Seek forgiveness for our sins and forgive people who have (purposely or innocently) offended us. Here is a scripture we should perhaps use for the first part. Psalm 51 is the result of the aftermath of Kind David's sin of adultery with Bathsheba. (See II Sam. 11:2-13) In his Psalm he relates what our attitude should be when approaching God for forgiveness.

Psalm 51:1-12 ... [[To the chief Musician, A Psalm of David, when Nathan the prophet came unto him, after he had gone in to Bathsheba.]]

1.) *Have mercy upon me, O God, according to thy lovingkindness: according unto the multitude of thy tender mercies blot out my transgressions.*

(2.) *Wash me throughly from mine iniquity, and cleanse me from my sin.*

(3.) *For I acknowledge my transgressions: and my sin is ever before me.*

(4.) *Against thee, thee only, have I sinned, and done this evil in thy sight: that thou mightest be justified when thou speakest, and be clear when thou judgest.*

(5) *Behold, I was shapen in iniquity; and in sin did my mother conceive me.*

(6) *Behold, thou desirest truth in the inward parts: and in the hidden part thou shalt make me to know wisdom.*

(7.) *Purge me with hyssop, and I shall be clean: wash me, and I shall be whiter than snow.*

(8.) *Make me to hear joy and gladness; that the bones which thou hast broken may rejoice.*

(9.) *Hide thy face from my sins, and blot out all mine iniquities.*

(10.) *Create in me a clean heart, O God; and renew a right spirit within me.*

(11.) *Cast me not away from thy presence; and take not thy holy spirit from me.*

(12.) *Restore unto me the joy of thy salvation; and uphold me with thy free spirit."*

Now for the second part we're going to pull out our biggest gun. How would you feel about the person or persons who were responsible for not just saying bad things about you, but giving you the worst beating anyone could give and then nailing you to a wooden cross? For most of us that would be a little bit more than an "offence." But Jesus provides the ultimate example of forgiveness and releasing someone from their sin.

Luke 23:34 ... *"Then said Jesus, Father, forgive (G836 Strong's) them; for they know not what they do. And they parted his raiment, and cast lots."*

WHAT DO YOU MEAN THEY DIDN'T KNOW WHAT THEY WERE DOING? ARE YOU SERIOUS!? The men who were responsible for his torture and death knew EXACTLY what they were doing (they just didn't know who they were doing it to).The false witnesses lied knowing Jesus was innocent, the priests and religious officials knew that Jesus hadn't done the things they said he did. The Roman soldiers who executed him were proficient at killing people through crucifixion. To them it was practically an art form to see how long they could keep someone alive on a cross! If you haven't noticed already the same word in Greek (G836) that Jesus used in his model prayer to his disciples was exactly the same one he used on the cross!

But yet Jesus released them from their "offences." He "let go" all the feelings of vengeance and frustration. I'm talking about the man Christ Jesus. Yes, he was God, but he was every bit as human as we are. So, if he can do it, we can do it. In fact, I think God requires it of us.

Remember one more time Mark 11:26 ... *"But if ye do not forgive, neither will your father which is in heaven forgive your trespasses."*

It should be easy right? Wrong. Many times, for us it takes both time and a daily process of prayer to get things set right in us. Also remember, prayer doesn't always change the situation or circumstance, but real prayer will change US. Then we can let go of everything that holds us in a snare or trap of perhaps self-pity or a convoluted sense of right or wrong.

David again gives a scripture we may want to include in our prayer time...

"Examine me, O Lord, and prove me; try my reins and my heart."
—Psalm 26:2

Why is this important? Because our desire for justification and revenge can hold us hostage. Sometimes God sees in us what we either don't want to see or can't see. That's why we must use this portion of our prayer time to make sure we release our sins to God and release offences of other people toward us.

James 3:5 ... *"Even so the tongue is a little member, and boasteth great things. Behold, how great a matter a little fire kindleth."*

In 1878 the Hatfield's and McCoy's is one of the most famous feuds in American history. Do you know the reason why at least 15 men lost their lives? A Pig.

Now we're following a model we have been praying for forty minutes ...

FIRST TEN MINUTES – RECOGNITION

SECOND TEN MINUTES – SUBMISSION

THIRD TEN MINUTES – PETITION

FOURTH TEN MINUTES - |CONFESSION

Chapter 35

Superficial Prayers

Phil. 4:6-7 ... (6) *"Be careful for nothing; but in every thing by prayer and supplication with thanksgiving let your requests be made known unto God.*

(7) And the peace of God, which passeth all understanding, shall keep your hearts and minds through Christ Jesus."

Prayer is like anything that requires daily attention. It can get so common that we fail to understand how powerful it is. Some people treat prayer as a 911 call, only using it absolutely when they need to and then some feel compelled to perhaps come to the point where they just go through the motions to satisfy what they feel is their duty or obligation to pray.

Prayer can become boring, a chore, a constant state of questions why things aren't happening like you want them to. But prayer isn't so you can get everything you want from God, prayer is forging, sometimes through hard work to hear that still small voice for the answer you need, not the answer you want.

One thing I do know. Everybody prays differently according to their personality and temperament. God knows it because He created us as individuals, so as individuals we may all approach God from the same direction but we might get there a little different. (NO, I'm not talking about doctrine, I'm talking about how we approach God in and through prayer.)

The Bible says It's not wise to compare ourselves among

ourselves, (II Cor. 10:12) so for me to compare my prayer life with anyone else's might be foolish.

The other thing I think I know is this. When I seek God in prayer, faithfully and humbly, God listens and He will respond according to His will.

The amount of time isn't quite as important as the quality of time that I give Him. The way I focus on Him is more important than what I ask Him for. The motive behind my prayer is more important than what I say with my voice. Each of us must find that place in prayer where we are communicating with God (both speaking and listening) and our expectation is the result of that communication, rather than seeing the evidence of an answered prayer.

There is both personal prayer and congregational prayer. The later can never take the place of a personal time of prayer. Both can be powerful and both are necessary.

There is also ...

Intercessory prayer

Travailing prayer

Petitions & Supplications

The prayer of faith

The prayer of Importunity

The prayer for healings

The prayer for deliverance

The prayer of the enemy

The prayer of desperation

The prayer of confidence

And the list could go on and on, in fact Herbert Lockyer wrote a book entitled *"All the prayers of the Bible."*

The most ineffectual prayer is the prayer that isn't prayed. And the most dangerous prayer isn't the prayer that isn't prayed, it's the superficial prayer... and that's easier to pray than perhaps we think...

Superficial means at or close to the surface, external or outward. It can also mean shallow, apparent rather than real, insubstantial or insignificant.

Isaiah 1:15 ... *"And when ye spread forth your hands, I will hide mine eyes from you: yea, when ye make many prayers, I will not hear: your hands are full of blood."*

I almost think that God is not obligated to answer a superficial prayer. Or rather He gives us superficial answers to our superficial prayers.

The bottom line is ... Superficial prayers are dangerous because they have no substance...

Or... Because they have no understanding ...

Or... Because they have no emotion or passion...

Or... Because they have no faith ... no authority ... and no power.

For roughly 2 years we have dedicated Sun. nights to prayer (and we will continue to do so) but for this year, we must look to ourselves and make sure we are seeking God daily, consistently, and faithfully.

God wants us to have revival in our city, but He also wants revival in this church. But more than that He wants us to have revival in our homes and in our own personal time with Him.

In fact, if we get revival in us, we'll get revival in our homes, church, city, state, & nation.

Chapter 36

"The Fool's Prayer"

1 Corinthians 4:10-16 ... (10) "We are fools for Christ's sake, but ye are wise in Christ; we are weak, but ye are strong; ye are honourable, but we are despised.

(11) Even unto this present hour we both hunger, and thirst, and are naked, and are buffeted, and have no certain dwellingplace;

(12) And labour, working with our own hands: being reviled, we bless; being persecuted, we suffer it:

(13) Being defamed, we intreat: we are made as the filth of the world, and are the offscouring of all things unto this day.

(14) I write not these things to shame you, but as my beloved sons I warn you.

(15) For though ye have ten thousand instructors in Christ, yet have ye not many fathers: for in Christ Jesus I have begotten you through the gospel.

(16) Wherefore I beseech you, be ye followers of me."

PLEASE DON'T BE OFFENDED, WHEN I SAY ...

Imbeciles, simpletons, stupid or dull, a blockhead, a schildburger in Netherlands, in Jewish Folklore a schlemiel or schlimazl, a numbskull, or a noodlehead is described as well-meaning folks who take advice too literally to their own grievance or who find the most complicated solution for the most-simple of problems.

(Like THE NEW MATH) There are wise & clever fools, licensed fools, natural fools, a holy fool ... you get the idea. Maybe the world is the ship of fools?

From Dictionary.com ...

Fool - Noun

- *a silly or stupid person; a person who lacks judgment or sense.*
- *a professional jester, formerly kept by a person of royal or noble rank for amusement: the court fool.*
- *a person who has been tricked or deceived into appearing or acting silly or stupid: to make a fool of someone. (The TV show)*
- *an ardent enthusiast who cannot resist an opportunity to indulge an enthusiasm*
- *a weak-minded or idiotic person.*

From Wikipedia ...

Ivan the Fool (Russian) or Ivan the Ninny is a lucky fool stock character who appears in Russian folklore, a very simple-minded, but, nevertheless, lucky young man. Ivan is described as a likeable fair-haired and blue-eyed youth.

The approximate setting of Ivan the Fool's adventures is the 15th or 16th century Russia.

When he appears in stories, Ivan the Fool is usually portrayed as either a peasant or the son of a poor family. He is usually the youngest of three brothers, and although they appear to be much smarter than he, they are sometimes unkind to and envious of him.

Unlike typical heroes, it is Ivan's simplicity and lack of guile that turn out to help him in his adventures. For example, he listens to his heart, rather than his mind, and he easily forgets offence and endeavors to help others even at his own expense. His naivety, kindness, and daring help him fight villains, make friends, win princesses' hearts, and ultimately he is rewarded with half a kingdom or some similar accomplishment.

The moral of these stories is that Ivan the Fool is rarely the fool, he is merely perceived as such by others owing to his simple nature and joviality. According to one theory, Ivan the Fool as he was originally created was not intended to be a fool at all. At that time the Russian word for (fool) did not have any negative connotation, and was used to refer to the youngest son in the family. It was only later that it obtained a new meaning, from which the ambiguity arose.

It is inevitably the case that he is a positive character in all tales that he is mentioned in.

SO, FOOL'S GET KIND OF A BAD RAP ...

And that's due partly because of the wisest man that ever lived. Solomon had quite a bit to say about the subject of fools.

Psalm 53:1 ... *"The fool hath said in his heart, There is no God. Corrupt are they, and have done abominable iniquity: there is none that doeth good."*

Prov. 10:18 ... *"He that hideth hatred with lying lips, and he that uttereth a slander, is a fool."*

Prov. 12:15 ... *"The way of a fool is right in his own eyes: but he that hearkeneth unto counsel is wise."*

Prov. 14:16 ... *"A wise man feareth, and departeth from evil: but the fool rageth, and is confident."*

Prov. 17:28 ... *"Even a fool, when he holdeth his peace, is counted wise: and he that shutteth his lips is esteemed a man of understanding."*

Ecc. 2:14 ... *"The wise man's eyes are in his head; but the fool walketh in darkness: and I myself perceived also that one event happeneth to them all."*

In fact, Solomon had a lot more to say about fools ... 36 scriptures in Proverbs, and 10 in Ecclesiastes.

BUT THINK ABOUT IT ...

A lot of the heroes of the Bible perhaps looked like fools as they lived their life in pursuit of God and His will ... sometimes being a fool isn't as bad as it sounds!

Abraham was a fool of faith, ... left his home, family, "Where're you going? "Out there!"

Sarah was a laughing fool, ... I mean come on having a baby at 91? Who wouldn't laugh?

Noah was a building fool, ... building a boat to save the world? Really?

Joseph was a dreaming fool, ... "you all are going to bow down to me!"

Abner died like a fool, ... he literally died within feet of safety.

"The Fool's Prayer"

Saul played the fool, ... by his own admission ... I Sam. 26:21

David was a Dancing fool, ... bringing the ark to Jerusalem ... "I will yet be more vile than thus, and will be base in my own sight ..."

Daniel was a praying fool, ... it was against the law to pray! 3 times a day by a open window!

Adino, Eleazar, & Shammah were fighting fools, ... 800 to 1; fought till his hand cleaved to his sword; defended a bean field all by himself.

Nabal was a fool's fool, ...his name literally means "fool" and it showed.

Shadrach, Meshach, & Abednego were standing fool's, ...when everybody else bowed down... "... we are not careful to answer thee in this matter."

Saul / Paul was a religious fool ... dragging men and women committing them to prison for believing in Christ.

But that same Paul became a fool of another kind ...

1 Cor. 3:18 ... "Let no man deceive himself. If any man among you seemeth to be wise in this world, let him become a fool, that he may be wise."

2 Cor. 11:22-28 ... (22) "Are they Hebrews? so am I. Are they Israelites? so am I. Are they the seed of Abraham? so am I.

(23) Are they ministers of Christ? (I speak as a fool) I am more; in labours more abundant, in stripes above measure, in prisons more frequent, in deaths oft.

(24) Of the Jews five times received I forty stripes save one.

(25) Thrice was I beaten with rods, once was I stoned, thrice I suffered shipwreck, a night and a day I have been in the deep;

(26) In journeyings often, in perils of waters, in perils of robbers, in perils by mine own countrymen, in perils by the heathen, in perils in the city, in perils in the wilderness, in perils in the sea, in perils among false brethren;

(27) In weariness and painfulness, in watchings often, in hunger and thirst, in fastings often, in cold and nakedness.

(28) Beside those things that are without, that which cometh upon me daily, the care of all the churches."

Paul's ministry defied every Jewish thing in him. He sacrificed a career, position, education, heritage, and culture. He literally threw away everything to gain a place in the kingdom of God of which he was self-proclaimed as chiefest of sinners. He became a servant and a slave of Christ. Nothing was more important, nothing else had greater preeminence, nothing was held back. And everyone said, He had it made! And he threw it away for the carpenter's son!

"What a fool!" And Paul said. Yep! That's me! A fool for Christ's sake!

"That's why I pray! That's why I'm willing to endure all these trials and tests! That's why I am willing to stand before Caesar and be judged!"

The Fool's Prayer
By Edward Rowland Sill

The royal feast was done; the King
Sought some new sport to banish care,
And to his jester cried: "Sir Fool,
Kneel now, and make for us a prayer!"

The jester doffed his cap and bells,
And stood the mocking court before;
They could not see the bitter smile
Behind the painted grin he wore.

He bowed his head, and bent his knee
Upon the monarch's silken stool;
His pleading voice arose: "O Lord,
Be merciful to me, a fool!

"No pity, Lord, could change the heart
From red with wrong to white as wool:
The rod must heal the sin; but, Lord,
Be merciful to me, a fool!

"'T is not by guilt the onward sweep
Of truth and right, O Lord, we stay;
'T is by our follies that so long
We hold the earth from heaven away.

"These clumsy feet, still in the mire,
Go crushing blossoms without end;
These hard, well-meaning hands we thrust
Among the heart-strings of a friend.

"The ill-timed truth we might have kept—
Who knows how sharp it pierced and stung!
The word we had not sense to say—
Who knows how grandly it had rung!

"Our faults no tenderness should ask,
The chastening stripes must cleanse them all;
But for our blunders—oh, in shame
Before the eyes of heaven we fall.

"Earth bears no balsam for mistakes;
Men crown the knave, and scourge the tool
That did his will; but Thou, O Lord,
Be merciful to me, a fool."

The room was hushed; in silence rose
The King, and sought his gardens cool,
And walked apart, and murmured low,
"Be merciful to me, a fool!"

The one thing about a fool that we should embrace totally and completely is that a fool just doesn't care what anybody else thinks about them. So, in that regard, I want to live for God, pray to God, praise and worship God publicly, preach, testify & teach, etc.

AND BECOME THE BEST FOOL I CAN BE!
THE FOOL FOR CHRIST!

Chapter 37

"The Lord's Prayer"

Part VI

Matthew 6:9-13 / Luke 11:2-4

(9) "After this manner therefore pray ye: Our Father which art in heaven, Hallowed be thy name.

(10) Thy kingdom come. Thy will be done in earth as it is in heaven.

(11) Give us this day our daily bread.

(12) And forgive us our debts, as we forgive our debtors.

(13) And lead us not into temptation, but deliver us from evil: for thine is the kingdom, and the power, and the glory, for ever. Amen."

INTRODUCTION

Edward McKendree Bounds, perhaps better known as E. M. Bounds was born in 1835 in Shelbyville, Missouri. At the age of 19 he became the youngest practicing lawyer in Missouri. At age 24 he was ordained into the Methodist church and became pastor of the assembly in Monticello, Missouri.

But the most notable thing about his ministry was his prayer life. After being held as a prisoner during the Civil War and suffering a serious head wound by a saber, he once again served as a pastor and instituted weekly prayer sessions lasting several hours leading his county into a spiritual revival. This was no doubt born from his commitment of rising at 4:00 a.m. each day and praying till 7:00 a.m.

It was said of this man that, *"Not a foolish word did we ever hear him utter. He was one of the most intense eagles of God that ever penetrated the ether."* His experience in prayer prompted him to pen no less than eleven books on prayer before his death in 1913 at the age of 78 years. Nine of those books weren't published until after his passing by his grandson and all eleven books are still in publication almost 100 hundred years later. What made him so different? He didn't just preach about prayer. He didn't just teach about prayer. He practiced prayer and made it a prominent part of his life. It was said of his early morning prayer time that... *he cared not for the protests of other occupants of his room at being awakened so early. No man could have made more melting appeals for lost souls and backslidden ministers than did Bounds. Tears ran down his face as he pleaded for us all in the room.* (Source – Wikipedia)

My question is this. Will this generation pass without an E. M. Bounds? Or a Leonard Ravenhill? An Andrew Murray, a Charles Finney, or a David Brainerd? Prayer for us must be something more than a ritual. True powerful prayer must go beyond the normal, because true prayer goes beyond the normal.

"Prayer is a trade to be learned. We must be apprentices and serve our time at it. Painstaking care, much thought, practice and labour are required to be a skillful tradesman in praying."

"We can do nothing without prayer. It surmounts or removes

all obstacles, overcomes every resisting force and gains its ends in the face of invincible hindrances in prayer"

"Trouble and prayer are closely related... Trouble often drives men to God in prayer, while prayer is the voice of men in trouble."

"Private place and plenty of time are the life of prayer."

—Quotes by E.M. Bounds

THE FIFTH TEN MINUTES

(13) And lead us not into temptation, but deliver us from evil: ....

The first forty minutes using the Lord's Prayer as a formula has taken us through **recognition**, then **submission**, followed by a time of **petition**, and making honest **confession** for our sins and letting go of the offences.

Now we will enter into a time of **preparation**. According to the word of God every man that wears a skin suit will at some time, and on numerous occasions, from various sources, will all be tempted in some way shape or form.

I Corinthians 10:13 ... *"There hath no temptation taken you but such as is common to man: but God is faithful, who will not suffer you to be tempted above that ye able; but will with the temptation also make a way to escape, that ye may be able to bear it."*

II Peter 2:9 ... *"The Lord knoweth how to deliver the godly out of temptations, and to reserve the unjust unto the day of judgment to be punished."*

James 1:13 ... *"Let no man say when he is tempted, I am tempted of God: for God cannot be tempted with evil, neither tempteth he any man."*

I guess the next question is this ... what does preparation have to do with temptation? Well Johnny here it is... If you knew someone was going smack you in the head with a rock, a board, whatever, what would you do? Find something to protect your head right? You would prepare yourself. So if the Word tells us we will be tempted, what do you do? It only makes sense for us to prepare ourselves for whenever, wherever, and however that may occur.

So how do we prepare for temptations? The Word of God itself is without a doubt one of our greatest weapons and protection...

Psalm 119:9 ... *"Wherewithal shall a young man cleanse his way? By taking heed thereto according to thy word."*

James 1:21 ... *"Wherefore lay apart all filthiness and superfluity of naughtiness, and receive with meekness the engrafted word* (implanted – in other words it's not there by chance or accidently. You're prepared!), *which is able to save your souls."*

Read Matthew 4:1- 11

(vs. 2) ... when he had fasted forty days and nights, ... Why? He was preparing himself!

(3) And when the tempter came...

*(4) **"It is written, ..."***

*(7) **"It is written again, ..."***

*(10) **"Get thee hence, Satan: for it is written..."***

(11) "Then the devil leaveth him, and, behold, angels came and ministered unto him."

Three times on this occasion the devil tempted Jesus. Three times he resisted the temptation by using the word of God. You see the devil may have a measure of power but ultimately God's word trumps any temptation, IF WE'VE PREPARED OURSELVES.

THE BOY SCOUTS GOT IT

In days gone by I was in the Boy Scouts. I will never forget their simple yet powerful motto... BE PREPARED. And God expects those who love him and are striving to live for Him to be ***prepared*** also. We must be equipped with the things that will enable us to not just resist the devil, but also from all temptations. Know this. Temptation from sin doesn't always come from the devil...

James 1:14 ... *"But every man is tempted, when he is drawn away of his own lust, and enticed."*

So, the preparations we will make defend us not just against old slew-foot but even helps us keep our own desires pure and Godly. So let's find the equipment available in God's word to prepare us for the conflict to come!

Read Romans 13:11-14

(12) "...let us therefore cast off the works of darkness, and put on the armour of light.

(14) "But put ye on the Lord Jesus Christ, and make not provision for the flesh, to fulfill the lusts thereof."

Protection is preparation. By putting on the armor of God we are preparing for the inevitable. But isn't armor a little extreme? Isn't it a little inconvenient? Well if you think so go play full contact football with the Tennessee Titans without any helmet or pads. You think you might get hurt? (No answer needed.) Paul writes to the Ephesian church about it in chapter six.

Read Ephesians 6:10-18)

(10) "Finally, my brethren, be strong in the Lord, and in the power of his might.

(11) Put on the whole armor of God, that ye may be able to stand against the wiles (methods) of the devil.

(13) Wherefore take unto you the whole armor of God, that ye

may be able to withstand in the evil day, and having done all, to stand."

Larry Lea's lesson on preparation ...

WE ARE CLAIMING THE PROMISES OF GOD

When we put on the spiritual armor we are declaring confidence in His protection and the power of His promises.

(vs.14) *",having your loins gird about with truth,..."* When we put on the belt of truth we are declaring that, ... *"Jesus is my Truth."*

The Promise ... *"I am the way, the truth, and the life: no man cometh unto the Father, but by me ."* —John 14:6

(vs. 14) *"and having the breastplate of righteousness; ..."* When we put on the chest protection we are preparing to protect our heart and we are declaring that, ... *"Jesus is my Righteousness."*

The Promise ... *"For he hath made him to be sin for us, who knew no sin; that we might be made the righteousness of God in him."* —I Corinthians 5:21

(vs.15) *"And your feet shod with the preparation of the gospel of peace; ..."* When you put your gospel shoes on you are prepared to go anywhere He may lead you. You are declaring that, ... *"Jesus you are my Readiness."*

The Promise ... *"For thou hast delivered my soul from death: wilt not thou deliver my feet from falling, that I may walk before God in the light of the living?* —Psalm 56:13

(vs. 16) *"...taking the shield of faith, wherewith ye shall be able to quench all the fiery darts of the wicked."* When you take hold of the shield of faith your declaring ... *"Jesus, you are my faith.*

The Promise ... *"The God of my rock; in him will I trust: he is my* *shield, and the horn of my salvation, my high tower, and my refuge, my salvation; thou savest me from violence."* —II Samuel 22:3

(vs. 17) "And take the helmet of salvation,... " When I put on the helmet of salvation to prepare and protect my mind then I am declaring that, ... "Jesus is my Salvation."

The Promise *... And being made perfect, he became the author of eternal salvation unto all them that obey him; ..."* —Hebrews 5:9

(vs. 17) "... and the sword of the Spirit, which is the word of God:" When you claim and declare the sword of the Spirit you are saying, "Jesus is my living Word."

The Promise *... "For the word of God is quick and powerful, and sharper than any twoedged sword, piercing even to the dividing asunder of soul and spirit, and of the joints and marrow, and is a discerner of the thoughts and intents of the heart."* —Hebrews 4:12

CONCLUSION

Prayer gives us many things, but if we are to go into a dark, perverse, unsaved world filled with dangers and temptations let's get prepared. You WILL be tested, you WILL be tried, you WILL be tempted. So maybe we ought to take a few minutes and get prepared.

FIRST TEN MINUTES – RECOGNITION
SECOND TEN MINUTES – SUBMISSION
THIRD TEN MINUTES – PETITION
FOURTH TEN MINUTES – CONFESSION
FIFTH TEN MINUTES - PREPARATION

Chapter 38

The Problem with Prayer

1 Samuel 12:19-25 ... NKJV (19) *"And all the people said to Samuel, "Pray for your servants to the LORD your God, that we may not die; for we have added to all our sins the evil of asking a king for ourselves."*

(20) Samuel said to the people, "Do not fear. You have done all this wickedness; yet do not turn aside from following the LORD, but serve the LORD with all your heart.

(21) "And do not turn aside; for then you would go after empty things which cannot profit or deliver, for they are nothing.

(22) "For the LORD will not forsake His people, for His great name's sake, because it has pleased the LORD to make you His people.

(23) "Moreover, as for me, far be it from me that I should sin against the LORD in ceasing to pray for you; but I will teach you the good and the right way.

(24) "Only fear the LORD, and serve Him in truth with all your heart; for consider what great things He has done for you.

(25) "But if you still do wickedly, you shall be swept away, both you and your king."

James 4:1-3 ... NKJV (1) *"Where do wars and fights come from among you? Do they not come from your desires for pleasure that war in your members?*

(2) You lust and do not have. You murder and covet and cannot obtain. You fight and war. Yet you do not have because you do not ask.

(3) You ask and do not receive, because you ask amiss, that you may spend it on your pleasures."

"The problem with prayer is not that God doesn't answer our prayers, the problem is the prayers that are never prayed. Or the Prayers prayed the wrong way" —D. M. -03/28/2021

So, if you're not hearing something from God when you pray there are at least two obvious reasons why. You're not praying or you're not praying the right way. Yes, there are times in which God may remain silent to test you in some way, but the God that I read and study about in the Bible responds to the human practice of consistent prayer.

Another failure we have is realizing the importance or the priority that prayer must occupy in order to provoke us into a place of power and holiness. Here's the deal. We want God's blessing and fellowship on our terms, on our timetable, and at our convenience.

From a Barna Research Study

...Silent and Solo: How Americans Pray - August 2017

Prayer is not only the most common faith practice among American adults (79% have prayed at least once in the past three months), it's also one of the most complex and multifaceted.

How Do You Most Often Pray?

The forces of our individualistic culture have influenced what was once a more communal and corporate conception of Christian identity to one now focused primarily on the individual. This "personal" faith focus plays out most explicitly in the practice of prayer: almost all American adults (94%) who have prayed at least once in the last three months most often choose to pray by themselves. Not only are most prayers a solo practice, but the vast majority are also most often silent (82% compared to 13% audible and solo prayers). Affirming this shift is the fact that only a very small percentage most often pray audibly with another person or group (2%), or collectively with a church (2%).

What Is the Content of Your Prayers?

American adults who pray with regularity do so with varying motivations, the most common being to offer "gratitude and thanksgiving" (62%). Generationally, this is lowest among Millennials (53%) and highest among Boomers (71%). An equally popular prayer incentive is the "needs of their family and community" (61%), followed by "personal guidance in crisis" (49%). The latter is most common among those with lower levels of education (49% with a high school diploma or less, compared to 39% of college graduates).

Although the article is extensive and informative the most telling thing to me is, that at least a portion of Americans are satisfied with the Lone Ranger approach to prayer. You know the strong silent type. Man of few words. But the reality is we need more verbal communal communication with our King!

In other words, silent and solo doesn't get the job done! Why do we feel like we must pray silent prayers? The world is screaming in our face what they want to say. Why should the church of the living God remain silent? And why should we settle for the solo act of prayer? In practically every other endeavor in life unity and community brings more effectiveness in affecting our world. Why do we insist on the Hans Solo approach to prayer? If the physical body cannot operate without the other members, how will the spiritual body operate without the other members?

Top Three Reasons People Don't Pray - June 27, 2012 |

The instructor's voice was gentle and soothing as she explained the final stretches before the end of the workout. "These may be the only three minutes of quiet you have all day; so take this time to be still." She walked to the back of the room and switched the lights off. The room was silent except for the music and the sound of her voice.

At first, every part of me wanted to jump to my feet and head out the door. After all, the clock was ticking away precious minutes and I had a list of chores calling me.

But I leaned back onto the blue foam mat alongside 20 other sweating, or should I say glowing, ladies in the Barre Class. Someone had given us permission—not just permission, but instruction—to hush and be still. In the following weeks, this became my favorite moment in the hour-long exercise class.

Those words sunk in: "the only minutes in your day you have to stop and be still." So <u>I'm thinking about prayer this morning. Listening and worshipping, praising and petitioning our Heavenly Father is, sadly for some, barely three minutes tagged on at the end of a busy day</u>. Sigh..."Lord forgive me, bless me, and good night!" does not make for a rich prayer life.

How often we excuse ourselves, thinking these few moments are all we can afford to give. After all, who knows exactly how much time we devote to prayer, praise, and petition? We'd rather not know. But God does.

Now don't jump up and head out the door just yet; it's time to think about this for just a few more minutes. Why is it that we neglect to pray? I suspect most of us don't pray because:

We don't think we have time.

We don't think it is important.

We don't believe that it makes any difference.

First of all, we do have the time! According a recent article in The Wall Street Journal, a Neilson Study reported that in 2010, Americans spend 63.5 billion minutes on social networks and blogs. How much time do you spend on social networks like Facebook? Another Nielson study indicates that an average Internet user spends 68 hours on the Internet per month, about 2 hours and 6 minutes per day. I rest my case; we do have the time to pray. As someone put it recently, "One of the great uses of Twitter and Facebook will be to prove at the Last Day that prayerlessness was not from lack of time."4

Secondly, prayer is necessary! We know that while He was on earth, Jesus was dependent on spending vital time in prayer with the Father. How much more should we? Hebrews 5:7 reveals the passionate prayer life of our Lord. During the days of Jesus' life on earth, He offered up prayers and petitions with loud cries and tears to the One who could save Him from death, and He was heard because of His reverent submission.

Before you think that you don't need to take time to pray, think of the staggering defeat of the Israelite army when they went up to fight against the little city called Ai. Confident with victory over the mighty fortress of Jericho, they neglected to pray and consult the Lord before going to battle. Bold and careless, they were soundly defeated.

Lastly, prayer does make a difference! As Greg has often quoted, prayer is "not for getting man's will done in heaven, but for getting God's will done on earth."

Prayer's not magic; it isn't simply submitting a grocery list to God. Remember that our Father is in heaven and we are on earth. But as His children, we can be confident that He wants to bless, use, guide, and provide for us. Perhaps "you have not because you ask not."

How is your prayer life? Don't you realize that what breathing is to our physical lives, prayer is to our spiritual lives?

The Problem with prayer is how God responds to the prayers we manage to pray. The problem with prayer is convincing ourselves that it's worth the sacrifice and effort.

Chapter 39

The Altar of Incense

Exodus 30:1 -10 NKJV

(1) "You shall make an altar to burn incense on; you shall make it of acacia wood.

(2) "A cubit shall be its length and a cubit its width—it shall be square—and two cubits shall be its height. Its horns shall be of one piece with it.

(3) "And you shall overlay its top, its sides all around, and its horns with pure gold; and you shall make for it a molding of gold all around.

(4) "Two gold rings you shall make for it, under the molding on both its sides. You shall place them on its two sides, and they will be holders for the poles with which to bear it.

(5) "You shall make the poles of acacia wood, and overlay them with gold.

(6) "And you shall put it before the veil that is before the ark of the Testimony, before the mercy seat that is over the Testimony, where I will meet with you.

(7) "Aaron shall burn on it sweet incense every morning; when he tends the lamps, he shall burn incense on it.

(8) "And when Aaron lights the lamps at twilight, he shall burn incense on it, a perpetual incense before the LORD throughout your generations.

(9) "You shall not offer strange incense on it, or a burnt offering, or a grain offering; nor shall you pour a drink offering on it.

(10) "And Aaron shall make atonement upon its horns once a year with the blood of the sin offering of atonement; once a year he shall make atonement upon it throughout your generations. It is most holy to the LORD."

PRAYER TO GOD WAS NEVER MEANT TO BE AN UNORGANIZED & UNDISCIPLINED RANDOM EVENT ...

The Creator of the Universe is a God of order and never does anything by accident or pure emotion. And prayer for us should follow the same model. At first glance prayer is the outpouring of our inner man. Which admittedly includes our feelings and emotions, but prayer is meant to be orderly and upright and disciplined.

"A farmer is helpless to grow grain; all he can do is provide the right conditions for the growing of grain. He cultivates the ground, he plants the seed, he waters the plants, and then the natural forces of the earth take over and up comes the grain...This is the way it is with the Spiritual Disciplines - they are a way of sowing to the Spirit... By themselves the Spiritual Disciplines can do nothing; they can only get us to the place where something can be done."

— Richard J. Foster, Celebration of Discipline:
The Path to Spiritual Growth

"Of all spiritual disciplines prayer is the most central because it ushers us into perpetual communion with the Father."

— Richard J. Foster, *Celebration of Discipline:*
The Path to Spiritual Growth

To pray is to change. All who have walked with God have viewed prayer as the main business of their lives.

For those explorers in the frontiers of faith, prayer was no little habit tacked on to the periphery of their lives; it was their lives. It was the most serious work of their most productive years. Prayer – nothing draws us closer to the heart of God.

— Richard J. Foster, *Celebration of Discipline:*
The Path to Spiritual Growth

"Simple Prayer involves ordinary people bringing ordinary concerns to a loving and compassionate Father. There is no pretense in Simple Prayer. We do not pretend to be more holy, more pure, or more saintly than we actually are. We do not try to conceal our conflicting and contradictory motives from God—or ourselves. And in this posture we pour out our heart to the God who is greater than our heart and who knows all things (1 John 3:20)."

— Richard J. Foster, *Prayer:*
Finding the Heart's True Home

TYPES AND SHADOWS OF THE ALTAR OF INCENSE

The Altar of Incense in the Tabernacle is unique because it represents the prayers and praise of God's people before His Mercy Seat... It was one of two altars that were part of the Tabernacle and its furnishings... the other was the Brasen Altar of Sacrifice. Both were necessary and vital to their worship and acceptance by God.

SIDE BY SIDE COMPARISON ...

Exodus 27 Altar of Sacrifice / Brazen Altar

Made of wood overlaid with brass or copper – symbolizes God's Righteous Judgement

The first thing when you entered the Tabernacle

A place where the innocent took the place of the guilty.

It had four horns where blood was shed for redemption and forgiveness

It took fire to consume the sacrifice.

A place of continual burning

Wood overlaid with brass

A place of death / blood. Everyday.

A place where things are laid down.

Transported – carried by the Priests

A Symbol of Salvation and repentance

Exodus 30 - Altar of Incense

Made of wood overlaid with gold – symbolizes glory & holiness

The last thing before you entered the presence of God.

A place where the priest left his will and his pride.

It had four horns where blood was applied for purity and cleansing. Atonement / Reconciliation

It took fire to produce the sweet-smelling savour.

A place of continual burning.

A place of worship and praise and petition. Everyday.

A place where things are lifted up.

Transported – carried by the Priests

A Symbol of Prayer, Praise and Intercession

"Lord . . . give ear unto my voice . . . Let my prayer be set forth before thee as incense [and the lifting up of my hands as the evening sacrifice.]" (Psalm 141:1–2).

THE INCENSE

Exo 30:34-38 ... (34) *"And the LORD said to Moses: "Take sweet spices, stacte and onycha and galbanum, and pure frankincense with these sweet spices; there shall be equal amounts of each.*

(35) "You shall make of these an incense, a compound according to the art of the perfumer, salted, pure, and holy.

(36) "And you shall beat some of it very fine, and put some of it before the Testimony in the tabernacle of meeting where I will meet with you. It shall be most holy to you.

(37) "But as for the incense which you shall make, you shall not make any for yourselves, according to its composition. It shall be to you holy for the LORD.

(38) "Whoever makes any like it, to smell it, he shall be cut off from his people."

One commentator says, ... *that the type of incense used on the altar was also symbolic, making this sacred space a "fragrant and purified atmosphere similar to that enjoyed by Jehovah in heaven."* In other words, incense burning would make the holy place welcome for Jehovah to visit and make his divine presence known.

Its components were to stay the same perpetually, not just a sweet smell but to please God himself and draw Him to the Mercy Seat.

Prayer must be consistently offered up every day in a consistent manner.

The Altar of Incense is an O.T. type and shadow of N.T. Prayer and praise. It wasn't an optional activity performed by the priests when it was convenient or when they needed to because of circumstance.

The ritual of burning the incense everyday was a commandment by God just like the blood sacrifices were on the Brasen Altar. The word used in Ex. 30:8 pertaining to the altar of Incense is ... *perpetual.*

In Strong's Concordance that word literally means continuously, or constant. This well may have been in the back of the Apostle Paul's mind when he simply said in the epistle to the church in Thessalonica ... Pray without ceasing. I Thess. 5:17

NLT ... *Never stop praying*

NIV ... *pray continually*

NET ... *constantly pray*

Amplified ... *"Be unceasing in prayer [praying perserveringly];"*

My first question is ... When during our day is it when we don't need prayer?

Or maybe my question should be ... When during our day is when we don't need to be in direct contact with our Creator and Savior? I guess it's not just a matter of *needing to*, but *wanting to.*

We may not be able to physically or consciously pray 24 hours a day, but we should seek a place in prayer where we are in a constant attitude of prayerfulness.

WHY? BECAUSE I WANT TO!

"And when he had taken the book, the four beasts and four and twenty elders fell down before the Lamb, having every one of them harps, and golden vials full of odors [Greek incense], which are the prayers of saints." (Rev. 5:8)

Chapter 40

The Prayer of Authority

Every Sunday you only get a small piece of the pie. That's my job. Your job is to take what you're given and add it to what you've already received. If you received the whole pie at once, you'd get sick, you wouldn't be able to receive it So here's just another piece.

Exodus 14:10-23 (NKJV)

(10) "And when Pharaoh drew near, the children of Israel lifted their eyes, and behold, the Egyptians marched after them. So they were very afraid, <u>and the children of Israel cried out to the LORD</u>.

(11) Then they said to Moses, "Because there were no graves in Egypt, have you taken us away to die in the wilderness? Why have you so dealt with us, to bring us up out of Egypt?

(12) "Is this not the word that we told you in Egypt, saying, 'Let us alone that we may serve the Egyptians'? For it would have been better for us to serve the Egyptians than that we should die in the wilderness."

(13) And Moses said to the people, "Do not be afraid. Stand still, and see the salvation of the LORD, which He will accomplish for you today. For the Egyptians whom you see today, you shall see again no more forever.

(14) "The LORD will fight for you, and you shall hold your peace."

(15) And the LORD said to Moses, "<u>Why do you cry to Me? Tell the children of Israel to go forward</u>.

(16) "<u>But lift up your rod, and stretch out your hand over the sea and divide it. And the children of Israel shall go on dry ground through the midst of the sea.</u>

(17) "And I indeed will harden the hearts of the Egyptians, and they shall follow them. So I will gain honor over Pharaoh and over all his army, his chariots, and his horsemen.

(18) "Then the Egyptians shall know that I am the LORD, when I have gained honor for Myself over Pharaoh, his chariots, and his horsemen."

(19) And the Angel of God, who went before the camp of Israel, moved and went behind them; and the pillar of cloud went from before them and stood behind them.

(20) So it came between the camp of the Egyptians and the camp of Israel. Thus it was a cloud and darkness to the one, and it gave light by night to the other, so that the one did not come near the other all that night.

(21) <u>Then Moses stretched out his hand over the sea; and the LORD caused the sea to go back by a strong east wind all that night, and made the sea into dry land, and the waters were divided</u>.

(22) So the children of Israel went into the midst of the sea on the dry ground, and the waters were a wall to them on their right hand and on their left.

(23) And the Egyptians pursued and went after them into the midst of the sea, all Pharaoh's horses, his chariots, and his horsemen."

From Dictionary.com …

Authority - *the power to determine, adjudicate (to pronounce or decree judicial decree), or otherwise settle issues or disputes; jurisdiction; the right to control, command, or determine.*

I guess the question isn't necessarily what you're praying, it's HOW you're praying.

Are you crying out like a captive slave or praying like a son with all the authority, rights, promises and privileges of their Father?

You have a promise with God so pray like it! You have a position with God so pray like it! You have an inheritance with God so pray like it! You have the name that is above every name so pray like it! You have the Word of God in your hearts so pray like it! You have the power of the Holy Ghost in you so pray like it!

We need to quit praying like a bunch of whiny captive slaves and start praying like blood bought empowered sons and daughters of the Almighty God!

Prov. 29:2 (NKJV) ... *"When the righteous are in authority, the people rejoice; But when a wicked man rules, the people groan."*

Luke 10:19 (NKJV) ... *"Behold, I give you the authority to trample on serpents and scorpions, and over all the power of the enemy, and nothing shall by any means hurt you."*

Chapter 41

The Sinner's Prayer

Psalm 51:1-19 ... KJV (1) *[[To the chief Musician, A Psalm of David, when Nathan the prophet came unto him, after he had gone in to Bathsheba.]] Have mercy upon me, O God, according to thy lovingkindness: according unto the multitude of thy tender mercies blot out my transgressions.*

(2) Wash me throughly from mine iniquity, and cleanse me from my sin.

(3) For I acknowledge my transgressions: and my sin is ever before me.

(4) Against thee, thee only, have I sinned, and done this evil in thy sight: that thou mightest be justified when thou speakest, and be clear when thou judgest.

(5) Behold, I was shapen in iniquity; and in sin did my mother conceive me.

(6) Behold, thou desirest truth in the inward parts: and in the hidden part thou shalt make me to know wisdom.

(7) Purge me with hyssop, and I shall be clean: wash me, and I shall be whiter than snow.

(8) Make me to hear joy and gladness; that the bones which thou hast broken may rejoice.

(9) Hide thy face from my sins, and blot out all mine iniquities.

(10) Create in me a clean heart, O God; and renew a right spirit within me.

(11) Cast me not away from thy presence; and take not thy holy spirit from me.

(12) Restore unto me the joy of thy salvation; and uphold me with thy free spirit.

(13) Then will I teach transgressors thy ways; and sinners shall be converted unto thee.

(14) Deliver me from bloodguiltiness, O God, thou God of my salvation: and my tongue shall sing aloud of thy righteousness.

(15) O Lord, open thou my lips; and my mouth shall shew forth thy praise.

(16) For thou desirest not sacrifice; else would I give it: thou delightest not in burnt offering.

(17) The sacrifices of God are a broken spirit: a broken and a contrite heart, O God, thou wilt not despise.

(18) Do good in thy good pleasure unto Zion: build thou the walls of Jerusalem.

(19) Then shalt thou be pleased with the sacrifices of righteousness, with burnt offering and whole burnt offering: then shall they offer bullocks upon thine altar."

MUCH OF WHAT PASTORS DO IS ...

Simply reminding the saints what they should already know. We should know the scripture about *"All have sinned and come short of the glory of God."* Some are more faithful, some are more prayerful, some are more fruitful, some are more of this and less of that, but we all operate from the same platform of human flesh.

We can be a king or a priest, a prophet or a pastor or have no position at all, but we are all one in the condition of our thoughts or one act from being a sinner.

David was a man after God's own heart ... but you probably
   already knew that.

David was a skilled mighty man of war ... you know that.

He was a great king ... yeah man.

He excelled at worship & praise ... knew that too.

He was a giant killer ... Sunday school stuff.

He consulted the Ephod for God's direction ... yep you know

He wrote songs and could play the devil out of people...

He was the progenitor of the Messiah Jesus Christ...

He was the MAN ...

But he was a sinner ... and sinners need to pray. And he says or
sings in his psalm "Don't just forgive me, but wash me, cleanse
me, purge me, blot out my sins!"

The only thing that makes us saints instead of sinners is the
   sinners prayer!

The only thing that makes us kings & priests is the sinners
   prayer!

The only thing that makes us salt & light is the sinners
   prayer!

The only thing that makes us ambassadors of Christ is the
   sinners prayer!

The only thing that makes us Christians is the sinners
   prayer!

The only thing that makes us Apostles, Pastors, Prophets,
Teachers & Evangelists is the sinner's prayer!

The only thing that makes us to sit with Him in heavenly places
is the sinner's prayer!

And the only thing that makes the difference between heaven
and hell is the sinner's prayer!

Come on Church we are saints of the Most-High only because of the grace and mercy of God. And having the opportunity to pray a cleansing prayer of repentance!

Chapter 42

It Killed David Brainerd

Acts 20:17-24 ... (17) *"And from Miletus he sent to Ephesus, and called the elders of the church.*

(18) And when they were come to him, he said unto them, Ye know, from the first day that I came into Asia, after what manner I have been with you at all seasons,

(19) Serving the Lord with all humility of mind, and with many tears, and temptations, which befell me by the lying in wait of the Jews:

(20) And how I kept back nothing that was profitable unto you, but have shewed you, and have taught you publickly, and from house to house,

(21) Testifying both to the Jews, and also to the Greeks, repentance toward God, and faith toward our Lord Jesus Christ.

(22) And now, behold, I go bound in the spirit unto Jerusalem, not knowing the things that shall befall me there:

(23) Save that the Holy Ghost witnesseth in every city, saying that bonds and afflictions abide me.

*(24) **But none of these things move me, neither count I my life dear unto myself, so that I might finish my course with joy, and the ministry, which I have received of the Lord Jesus, to testify the gospel of the grace of God.**"*

A CAPSULE OF DAVID BRAINERD'S LIFE ...

David Brainerd was born on April 20, 1718 in Haddam, Connecticut, the son of Hezekiah, a Connecticut legislator, and Dorothy. He had nine siblings, one of whom was Dorothy's from a previous marriage. He was orphaned at the age of nine, as his father died in 1727 at the age of forty-six and his mother died five years later. (Wikipedia)

He was sent to live with one his nine siblings. He inherited a farm at age 19 but felt unsuited for farming and left to enroll in Yale University. On 12 July 1739, he recorded having an experience of 'unspeakable glory' that prompted in him a 'hearty desire to exalt [God], to set him on the throne and to "seek first his Kingdom." This has been interpreted by evangelical scholars as a conversion experience. Two months later, he enrolled at Yale. In his second year at Yale, he was sent home because he was suffering from a serious illness that caused him to spit blood. It is now believed that he was suffering from tuberculosis, the disease which would lead to his death seven years later.

In his second year at Yale, Brainerd was expelled because it was said that he commented that one of his tutors, Chauncey Whittelsey, 'has no more grace than a chair' and that he wondered why the Rector 'did not drop down dead' for fining students perceived as over-zealous. He later apologized for the first comment, but denied making the second. Wikipedia

On the 1st of April 1743, after a brief period serving a church on Long Island, Brainerd began working as a missionary to Native Americans, which he would continue until late 1746 when worsening illness prevented him from working. In his final years, he also suffered from a form of depression that was sometimes immobilizing and which, on at least twenty-two occasions, led him to wish for death. He was also affected by difficulties faced by other missionaries of the period, such as loneliness and lack of food.

—Wikipedia

From https://www.wholesomewords.org/missions/biobrain.html

Yet this young man, who would have been considered a real risk by any present-day mission board, became a missionary to the American Indians and, in the most real sense, "the pioneer of modern missionary work." Brainerd began his ministry with the Indians in April, 1743, at Kannameek, New York, then ministered in Crossweeksung and Cranberry, New Jersey. These were the areas of his greatest successes.

Brainerd's first journey to the Forks of the Delaware to reach that ferocious tribe resulted in a miracle of God that preserved his life and revered him among the Indians as a "Prophet of God." Encamped at the outskirts of the Indian settlement, Brainerd planned to enter the Indian community the next morning to preach to them the Gospel of Christ. Unknown to him, his every move was being watched by warriors who had been sent out to kill him. F.W. Boreham recorded the incident:

But when the braves drew closer to Brainerd's tent, they saw the paleface on his knees. And as he prayed, suddenly a rattlesnake slipped to his side, lifted up its ugly head to strike, flicked its forked tongue almost in his face, and then without any apparent reason, glided swiftly away into the brushwood. "The Great Spirit is with the paleface!" the Indians said; and thus they accorded him a prophet's welcome.

That incident in Brainerd's ministry illustrates more than the many Divine interventions of God in his life — it also illustrates the importance and intensity of prayer in Brainerd's life. Believe it — Brainerd prayed! Read the Life and Diary of David Brainerd. On page after page, one reads such sentences as:

Wednesday, April 21 ...and God again enabled me to wrestle for numbers of souls, and had much fervency in the sweet duty of intercession...

Lord's Day, April 25... This morning I spent about two hours in secret duties and was enabled more than ordinarily to agonize for immortal souls. Though it was early in the morning and the sun scarcely shined at all, yet my body was quite wet with sweat...

Saturday, December 15... Spent much time in prayer in the woods and seemed raised above the things of this world...

Monday, March 14 ...in the morning was almost continually engaged in ejaculatory prayer...

Thursday, August 4... Was enabled to pray much, through the whole day...

Thursday, November 3... Spent this day in secret fasting, and prayer, from morning till night...

Suffice it to say, it is not surprising to read then of the miraculous interventions of God on Brainerd's behalf, and of the mighty ministry and the unbelievable revivals he experienced among the iniquitous, idolatrous Indians in those short years. A volume such as this prohibits more than only mere mention of some of those supernal, supernatural scenes: "I have now baptized, in all, forty-seven persons of the Indians. Twenty-three adults and twenty-four children...Through rich grace, none of them as yet have been left to disgrace their profession of Christianity by any scandalous or unbelieving behavior" (Nov. 20, 1743). What pastor or evangelist reading this can say the same?

Lord's Day, December 29 ...After public worship was over, I went to my house, proposing to preach again after a short season of intermission. But they soon came in one after another; with tears in their eyes, to know, "what they should do to be saved..." It was an amazing season of power among them, and seemed as if God had "bowed the heavens and come down..." and that God was about to convert the whole world.

By the end of his short life, he had traveled 3,000 miles on horseback as a missionary to the American Indian. (Wikipedia)

His Diary and Journal are a brim with ministries and miracles that were akin to the acts of the Apostles. The Life and Diary of David Brainerd ought to be read — and read often — by God's people. It will do something for you spiritually. You will be convicted, challenged, changed, charged. It has had life-transforming effect upon many, motivating them to become missionaries, evangelists, preachers, people of prayer and power with God.

Brainerd died in 1747 (at the age of 29) in the home of Jonathan Edwards. His ministry to the Indians was contemporary with Wesley, Whitefield and Edwards as they ministered to the English-speaking people during the period called in English and American history, the "Great Awakening." Brainerd's centuries-spanning influence for revival is positive proof God can and will use any vessel, no matter how fragile and frail, if it is only sold out to souls and the Saviour!

It wasn't the traveling that killed David Brainerd ... 3,000 miles on horseback

It wasn't being orphaned at the age of nine...

It wasn't the shame and anxiety related to being kicked out of Yale University ...

It wasn't the tuberculosis that killed him ...

In 2016, there were more than 10 million cases of active TB which resulted in 1.3 million deaths.

It wasn't being subjected to harsh living conditions living with the Indians...

It wasn't the debilitating bouts of depression ...

IT WAS CARRYING A BURDEN FOR THE LOST AND PRAYER!

Reaching the lost, preaching the gospel under the most severe conditions, mentally, physically, and spiritually. You just might say that consistent, faithful, intercessory prayer killed David Barinerd.

WHAT A WAY TO GO!

Chapter 43

"Just Prayer"

James 5:13-18

(13) "Is any among you afflicted? let him pray. Is any merry? let him sing psalms.

(14) Is any sick among you? let him call for the elders of the church; and let them pray over him, anointing him with oil in the name of the Lord:

(15) And the prayer of faith shall save the sick, and the Lord shall raise him up; and if he have committed sins, they shall be forgiven him.

(16) Confess your faults one to another, and pray one for another, that ye may be healed. The effectual fervent prayer of a righteous man availeth much.

(17) Elias was a man subject to like passions as we are, and he prayed earnestly that it might not rain: and it rained not on the earth by the space of three years and six months.

(18) And he prayed again, and the heaven gave rain, and the earth brought forth her fruit."

Prayer is kind of like oxygen. You really don't think about it till you need it. You would think something so necessary, so vital, so powerful would take a place of greater place of priority in our lives.

Have you ever heard anyone say something like, "Well, all we can do is pray."

As if we have exhausted every other option, and it's the only thing left to do. As if it has become so common that it no longer is a privilege, precious or powerful. It has become ... Just prayer. Just a prayer meeting, just a common expected Christian activity, just a chore, just a less priority till we actually need it kind of thing.

According to Dictionary.com prayer is defined as ...

- a devout petition to God or an object of worship.
- a spiritual communion with God or an object of worship, as in supplication, thanksgiving, adoration, or confession.
- the act or practice of praying to God or an object of worship.

We read or hear that definition and we think, Yeah, I know it's just prayer.

Prayer to humanity is a little like opinions. We all have them but they're usually misinformed, misrepresented, and misunderstood.

Here are some more quotes about prayer... some are from a secular perspective and as such carry a human attitude. But I wanted to include more than just the Christian view of what prayer perhaps means to us ...

"The man who prays is the one who thinks that God has arranged matters all wrong, but who also thinks that he can instruct God how to put them right." —Christopher Hitchens

"And here's something else, another problem you might have: Suppose your prayers aren't answered. What do you say? "Well, it's God's will." "Thy Will Be Done." Fine, but if it's God's will, and He's going to do what He wants to anyway, why bother praying in

the first place? Seems like a big waste of time to me! Couldn't you just skip the praying part and go right to His Will? It's all very confusing." —George Carlin

"Why is it that when we talk to God we're said to be praying, but when God talks to us we're schizophrenic?" —Lily Tomlin

"I talk to God but the sky is empty." —Sylvia Plath

"Prayer is beyond any question the highest activity of the human soul. Man is at his greatest and highest when upon his knees he comes face to face with God." — D. Martyn Lloyd-Jones

Prayer is not an old woman's idle amusement. Properly understood and applied, it is the most potent instrument of action. —Mahatma Gandi

"Prayer may just be the most powerful tool mankind has." — Ted Dekker

I fear John Knox's prayers more than an army of ten thousand men. —Mary, Queen of Scotland

Prayer is submitting ourselves to the will, to the authority, and the timetable of God. —David Martin- 2018

People who truly pray hardly ever talk about it, they do it. —Me again

---

How Much Does Prayer Weigh?

Louise Redden, a poorly dressed lady with a look of defeat on her face, walked into a grocery store. She approached the owner of the store in a most humble manner and asked if he would let her charge a few groceries. She softly explained that her husband was very ill and unable to work, they had seven children and they needed food. John Longhouse, the grocer, scoffed at her and requested that she leave his store.

Visualizing the family needs, she said: 'Please, sir! I will bring you the money just as soon as I can."

John told her he could not give her credit, as she did not have a charge account at his store.

Standing beside the counter was a customer who overheard the conversation between the two. The customer walked forward and told the grocer man that he would stand good for whatever she needed for her family.

The grocer man said in a very reluctant voice, "Do you have a grocery list?"

Louise replied, "Yes sir."

"O.K." he said, put your grocery list on the scales and whatever your grocery list weighs, I will give you that amount in groceries."

Louise, hesitated a moment with a bowed head, then she reached into her purse and took out a piece of paper and scribbled something on it. She then laid the piece of paper on the scale carefully with her head still bowed. The eyes of the grocer man and the customer showed amazement when the scales went down and stayed down.

The grocerman staring at the scales, turned slowly to the customer and said begrudgingly, "I can't believe it." The customer smiled and the grocerman started putting the groceries on the other side of the scales. The scale did not balance so he continued to put more and more groceries on them until the scales would hold no more. The grocerman stood there in utter disgust.

Finally, he grabbed the piece of paper from the scales and looked *at it with greater amazement. It was not a grocery list, it was a prayer that said: "Dear Lord, you know my needs and I am leaving this in your hands."*

The grocerman gave her the groceries that he had gathered and placed on the scales and stood in stunned silence. Louise thanked him and left the store. The customer handed a fifty-dollar bill to John as he said, "It was worth every penny of it."

It was sometime later that John Longhouse discovered the scales were broken; therefore, only God knows how much a prayer weighs.

The Down Syndrome Miracle

One afternoon while walking through the lobby of a hotel in Grand Rapids, Michigan, I became aware of a disturbance in one corner of the room. I walked in that direction in that casual way we use to check out disturbances in public places without announcing our curiosity. A boy of about four was screaming and rolling around on the floor in some kind of a fit.

Several people were trying to help the parents control the child. A crowd was gathering. It was a bad situation.

Then the Lord spoke to me.

"I want you to pray with that boy for a complete healing," he said. It wasn't an audible voice. But I heard the Lord say this as clearly as I have ever heard anything.

I suspected that the boy had Downs' Syndrome. I was astonished. Down's Syndrome is a genetic defect that always causes moderate to severe mental impairment and physical disability. Every cell in that boy's body had an extra chromosome. Every one of the billions of cells in his body was defective, and I was supposed to pray for a complete healing.

But I had heard the Lord. I took a deep and uneasy breath and went over to the parents; I told them that I wanted to pray for their son. I wanted to imply that the idea was mine, not the Lord's, in case nothing happened when I prayed.

I put my hands on the child and prayed. He calmed down immediately. I was filled with a sense that at that moment the Lord began to restore him completely.

He was. In the weeks and months following that event, the boy's development accelerated. The doctors could not find any explanation for it. When they ran the tests they could find no trace of Down's Syndrome. I still hear from the parents telling me how well he is doing.

—Michael Scanlan, TOR Steubenville, Ohio

IT WAS "JUST PRAYER" ...

Acts 12:1-17 ... (1) Now about that time Herod the king stretched forth his hands to vex certain of the church.

(2) And he killed James the brother of John with the sword.

(3) And because he saw it pleased the Jews, he proceeded further to take Peter also. (Then were the days of unleavened bread.)

(4) And when he had apprehended him, he put him in prison, and delivered him to four quaternions of soldiers to keep him; intending after Easter to bring him forth to the people.

(5) Peter therefore was kept in prison: **but prayer was made without ceasing of the church unto God for him.**

(6) And when Herod would have brought him forth, the same night Peter was sleeping between two soldiers, bound with two chains: and the keepers before the door kept the prison.

(7) And, behold, the angel of the Lord came upon him, and a light shined in the prison: and he smote Peter on the side, and raised him up, saying, Arise up quickly. And his chains fell off from his hands.

(8) And the angel said unto him, Gird thyself, and bind on thy sandals. And so he did. And he saith unto him, Cast thy garment about thee, and follow me.

(9) And he went out, and followed him; and wist not that it was true which was done by the angel; but thought he saw a vision.

(10) When they were past the first and the second ward, they came unto the iron gate that leadeth unto the city; which opened to them of his own accord: and they went out, and passed on through one street; and forthwith the angel departed from him.

(11) And when Peter was come to himself, he said, Now I know of a surety, that the Lord hath sent his angel, and hath delivered me out of the hand of Herod, and from all the expectation of the people of the Jews.

(12) And when he had considered the thing, he came to the house of Mary the mother of John, whose surname was Mark; where many were gathered together praying.

(13) And as Peter knocked at the door of the gate, a damsel came to hearken, named Rhoda.

(14) And when she knew Peter's voice, she opened not the gate for gladness, but ran in, and told how Peter stood before the gate.

(15) And they said unto her, Thou art mad. But she constantly affirmed that it was even so. Then said they, It is his angel.

(16) But Peter continued knocking: and when they had opened the door, and saw him, they were astonished.

(17) But he, beckoning unto them with the hand to hold their peace, declared unto them how the Lord had brought him out of the prison. And he said, Go shew these things unto James, and to the brethren. And he departed, and went into another place."

IN OUR TEXT ...

It shows both the power of prayer and the weakness of human faith.

James 5:17 - New Living Translation

"Elijah was as human as we are, and yet when he prayed earnestly that no rain would fall, none fell for three and a half years!"

God doesn't expect us to shed our humanity to pray powerful prayers. But He does expect us to bring what we have and use it.

Besides Elijah's prayers in James ...

-   fire was called down from heaven. Three times!
-   a barrel of meal and a cruse of oil never went empty
-   a widow's dead son was resurrected.

And because of "Just Prayer" ...

-   Water came from the rock, manna was provided in the wilderness, clothes / shoes didn't wear out,
-   God gave barren women children.
-   the lame were healed, the lepers were cleansed, and the sick were made whole ...
-   deaf ears were unstopped, fevers broke, ...

In Numbers 11:2 Moses "Just Prayed" ... *"...and when Moses prayed unto the Lord, the fire was quenched."*

In 2 Chron. 7:1 king Solomon "Just Prayed" ... *"Now when Solomon had made an end of praying, the fire came down from heaven, and consumed the burnt offering and the sacrifices; and the glory of the LORD filled the house."*

In II Kings 6 Elisha the prophet & protégé of Elijah "Just Prayed" - that his servants spiritual vision was opened ... and the physical eyes of the enemy would be blinded.

Good king Hezekiah had an incurable disease in Isaiah 38 so he "Just Prayed" – and received fifteen more years of life.

Jonah the renegade and rebellious prophet of God "Just Prayed" – and got delivered from the belly of a fish.

AND THE LIST GOES ON ...

I have personally seen God heal the effects of Meningitis on the human brain of a child.

- cancers have been healed
- minds have been restored.
- spirits have been cast out.
- Angels have been dispatched with answers and healing in their wings, the sun stood still, sins have been forgiven and blotted out, the mouths of lions were stopped, the place where believers were assembled was shaken, chains fell off, prison doors were opened wide, seas were parted and storms were stilled, the check came in the mail, groceries were delivered to the front door, mercy and protection were given, grace and power poured out, poisonous snake bites were healed (Paul).

All these and more besides are evidence of ... "Just Prayer."

Knowing that intercessory prayer is our mightiest weapon and the supreme call for all Christians today, I pleadingly urge our people everywhere to pray. Believing that prayer is the greatest contribution that our people can make in this critical hour, I humbly urge that we take time to pray--to really pray. Let there

be prayer at sunup, at noonday, at sundown, at midnight--all
through the day. Let us all pray for our children, our youth, our
aged, our pastors, our homes. Let us pray for our churches. Let us
pray for ourselves, that we may not lose the word 'concern' out of
our Christian vocabulary. Let us pray for our nation. Let us pray
for those who have never known Jesus Christ and His redeeming
love, for moral forces everywhere, for our national leaders. Let
prayer be our passion. Let prayer be our practice.
—General Robert E. Lee

Chapter 44

"The Lord's Prayer"

Part VII

Mathew 6:9-13 / Luke 11:2-4

(9) *"After this manner therefore pray ye: Our Father which art in heaven, Hallowed be thy name.*

(10) *Thy kingdom come. Thy will be done in earth as it is in heaven.*

(11) *Give us this day our daily bread.*

(12) *And forgive us our debts, as we forgive our debtors.*

(13) *And lead us not into temptation, but deliver us from evil: For thine is the kingdom, and the power, and the glory, forever. Amen.*

INTRODUCTION

Our hour is almost over. Basically, only ten minutes remain of our hour of prayer. We have entered into our prayer closet with **recognition**. Then presented ourselves to God as a living sacrifice in **submission**. Made our requests known to him through our **petition**. Made sure our sins and offenses were made right through our time of **confession**. Put on the whole armor of God in **preparation** for our spiritual warfare. Now we can finish off with a season of **adoration**.

"For thine is the kingdom and the power and the glory, for ever. Amen."

Adoration. It is something we shower on someone we truly think highly of. It is no secret if you adore someone. You are animated, you are vocal, you are demonstrative. You just can't help yourself, your adoration affects your speech, your actions and your attitudes. This should be one the most natural part of our prayer time. When we start thinking about the goodness and the greatness of God, it ought to be almost automatic. The old expression is... "It's all over except the shouting." We have arrived to the place where we are designed to excel ...

Psalm 102:16-22 ... *"When the Lord shall build up Zion, he shall appear in his glory.*

(17) He will regard the prayer of the destitute (Stripped, naked), and not despise their prayer.

(18) **This shall be written for the generation to come: and the people which shall be created shall *praise the Lord."**

(19) For he looked down from the height of his sanctuary; from heaven did the Lord behold the earth;

(20) To hear the groaning of the prisoner; to loose those that are appointed to death;

(21) To declare the name of the Lord in Zion, and his praise in Jerusalem;

(22) When the people are gathered together, and the kingdoms, to serve the Lord."

THE LAST TEN MINUTES

It's called ***adoration***! You see by now I just can't contain it. I've got to express through my flesh what he's done with my soul! But let's start where we need to start. Adoration has three basic definitions...

1.) Act of paying honor, as to a divine being; worship.

 2.) Reverent homage.

 3.) Fervent and devoted love.

The type of praise mentioned in Ps. 102:18 has several meanings but it indicates an outward physical expression. Praise is simply our expression of our relationship with our God. It is so natural that nature can't help itself...

Psalm 19:1 ... *"To The Chief Musician, A Psalm of David. The heavens declare the glory of God; the firmament sheweth his handiwork."*

Psalm 114:4 & 6... (4) *"The mountains skipped like rams, and the little hills like lambs."*

 (6) *"Ye mountains, that ye skipped like rams; ye little hills, like lambs?"*

Psalm 65:13 ... *"The pastures are clothed with flocks; the valleys also clothed over with corn; they shout for joy, they also sing."*

Isaiah 49:13 ... *"Sing, O heavens; and be joyful, O earth; and break forth into singing, O mountains: for the Lord hath comforted his people, and will have mercy upon his afflicted."*

Isaiah 55:12 ... *"For ye shall go out with joy, and be led forth with peace: the mountains and the hills shall break forth before you into singing, and all the trees of the field shall clap their hands."*

Here's the thing. Nature obeys the Creator. It doesn't have a choice. Its hard-wired to show forth the praise of the one who spoke them into existence. They (the created things of nature) praise him by commandment, but our praise comes from a personal relationship with him. It's a choice, it's a privilege, its adoration! I don't have to, I want to! In fact, I feel compelled to do it simply because He is not just my Creator, but my Savior, my Redeemer, my Healer, my Protector, my Provider, my Everything!

IT'S YOUR TURN

Psalm 66:2 ... *"Sing forth the honor of his name:* **make his praise glorious** *(abundant)."*

I Peter 2:9 ... *"But ye are a chosen generation, a royal priesthood, an holy nation, a peculiar people; that ye should show forth (to make known by praising or proclaiming, to celebrate.) the praises of him who hath called you out of darkness into his marvelous light."*

If nature has a hard time being silent, then what's the matter with us? Hasn't God done anything for you? Didn't He do what nobody else could do? How can we NOT praise Him?

Luke 19:37-40 ... *"And when he was come nigh, even now at the descent of the mount of Olives, the whole multitude of the disciples began to rejoice and praise God with a* **loud** *voice for all the mighty works that they had seen;*

(38) Saying, Blessed be the King that cometh in the name of the Lord: peace in heaven, and glory in the highest.

(39) And some of the Pharisees from among the multitude said unto him, Master, rebuke thy disciples.

(40) And he answered and said unto them, I tell you that, **if these should hold their peace, the stones would immediately cry out."**

We are celebrating the goodness and greatness of God. It should be a time of demonstration. We are **showing God** our praise. We're acting out, we're acting up, we're pulling out all the stops, and we want God to know exactly how we feel!

In Psalm 102 verse 18 the word praise in the original Hebrew is *halal.* It is used over 100 times in the scripture to describe the way we should praise him in the last ten minutes. It means...

To be vigorously excited, to laud, boast, rave, to celebrate, to be clamorously foolish.

The one person who demonstrated this kind of praise the best has to be King David when he brought the Ark of God to Jerusalem...

II Samuel 6:4-5,14-16 ... *"And they brought it out of the house of Abinadab which was at Gibeah, accompanying the ark of God: and Ahio went before the ark.*

(5) And David and all the house of Israel played before the Lord on all manner of instruments made of fir wood, even on harps, and on psalteries, and on timbrels, and cornets, and cymbals."

(14) And David danced before the Lord with all his might; and David was girded with a linen ephod.

(15) So David and all the house of Israel brought up the ark of the Lord with **shouting**, *and* **the sound of the trumpet.**

(16) And as the ark of the Lord came into the city of David, Michal Saul's daughter looked through the window, and saw king **David leaping and dancing before the Lord**; *and she despised him in her heart."*

Let me make a few observations and comments. Let's be honest, when we were under the influence of worldly things there were times, you really didn't care who was watching and what they thought. You may have been under the influence??? People do all kinds of crazy things when they're under the influence. Well, aren't we under His influence? Hasn't he made us forget all the toil and heartache, and pain, and frustration without the hangover? Come on if we can get a little crazy and happy doing worldly stuff, shouldn't we get a little crazy and happy with God? The world doesn't feel the need to apologize for their manner of celebrations, so why should we? Who hasn't been driving in their car or got the stereo up real loud in the house, and all of sudden you just felt like dancing or singing like a karaoke pro? Come on admit it! The world isn't ashamed when they celebrate (Mardi Gras, New Year's Eve, Super Bowl Sunday, etc.) why should we be ashamed of making some noise for our God.

Let's briefly get back to David. This king of Israel just didn't care if anyone saw or heard him. He had found a place in God where he just didn't care what anyone thought of his worship. I think that's one thing God enjoyed about David. He celebrated the presence of God. It didn't matter who else was there, what anybody else was doing (or not doing), his desire was to give God the best of himself!

Round two. Now I want to point out to all the shy people who may not be ready to be too public with your worship. That's okay too. Remember, we are in our personal prayer time. We have spent 50 min. getting everything right with God and man. It's just you and HIM. So why not just let it rip! Let it out! Who cares? If you look totally silly, who cares? (It's just you and Him) If you're singing totally off key, so what? You know what the book of Psalms says?

Psalm 66:1 ... *To the Chief Musician, A Song or Psalm. "Make a joyful noise unto God, all ye lands:"*

Psalm 81:1 ... *To the chief Musician upon Gittith, A Psalm of Asaph. "Sing aloud unto God our strength: make a joyful noise unto the God of Jacob."*

Psalm 95:1-2 ... *"O come, let us sing unto the Lord: let is make a joyful noise to the rock of our salvation.*

(2) Let us come before his presence with thanksgiving, and make a joyful noise to the rock of our salvation."

Psalm 98:4 & 6 ... *"Make a joyful noise unto the Lord, all the earth: make a loud noise, and rejoice, and sing praise."*

(6) "With trumpets and sound of cornet make a joyful noise before the Lord, the King."

Psalm 100:1 ... *A Psalm of Praise. "Make a joyful noise unto the Lord, all ye lands."*

Seven times the scripture uses the term **"joyful noise."** The word "noise" there (H2135- Strong's) means, *"to split the ear, to shout a war-cry, to shout in triumph (Tarzan), to shout in applause, to shout for joy.* Wow, I think God is trying to tell us something. The number seven in scripture denotes "perfection." To the human ear a "joyful noise" may not be on any scale of music, but to God's ears... IT'S PERFECT! Why because you're not ashamed to celebrate what he has done to you, with you, and for you! Go ahead let it out! That's how the walls of Jericho came down! It's what they did when God did something great!

I believe the Church has remained timid and silent long enough! If we don't do it no one else will! (Listen for them rocks) Come on...

Psalm 47:1 ... *O clap your hands, all ye people; shout unto God with the voice of triumph."*

FIRST TEN MINUTES – RECOGNITION

SECOND TEN MINUTES – SUBMISSION

THIRD TEN MINUTES – PETITION

FOURTH TEN MINUTES – PREPARATION

FIFTH TEN MINUTES – CONFESSION

SIXTH TEN MINUTES – ADORATION

Now we have a model to pray one hour a day!

Chapter 45

The Symphony of Prayer

1 Chron. 15:16 ... *"And David spake to the chief of the Levites to appoint their brethren to be the singers with instruments of musick, psalteries and harps and cymbals, sounding, by lifting up the voice with joy."*

Matt. 18:19-20 ... (19) *"Again I say unto you, That if two of you shall agree on earth as touching any thing that they shall ask, it shall be done for them of my Father which is in heaven.*

(20) For where two or three are gathered together in my name, there am I in the midst of them."

I'LL ADMIT IT ...

Many moons ago I was a Barry Manilow fan. Didn't go to any of his concerts. Didn't join his fan club. But I did buy most all of his recordings. I would sit in my room with my stereo system with headphones on and do the karaoke before it was the karaoke, singing side by side with the MAN-I-LOW.

You may have never heard of him if you were born after 1980. But Barry Manilow started his career as a backup singer and writer of TV commercial jingles. You know like the Dr. Pepper song, or *"I am stuck on Band-Aid brand, cause Band-Aid's stuck on me!"* Among others.

But in the middle of all his "American Bandstand's,

The Symphony of Prayer

"Copacabana's" and those sappy love songs, there is one song that I found truly unique in what it says and how it can be applied to prayer.

It's a song called "One Voice." The song begins with Mr. Manilow singing by himself, acappela (that means without music). Then as the song progresses other voices join him, (the studio version is also him dubbed in on different tracks), and instruments begin to swell, violins, woodwinds, brass and percussion join gradually until by the end there is a crescendo of both voices singing and instruments playing! (Look it up on YouTube.)

AND YOU SAY, "WHAT DOES THAT HAVE TO DO WITH PRAYER?"

And I'm thinking wow! Not because Barry Manilow is so talented but because it illustrates perfectly the spiritual principle that Jesus is talking about in Matthew 18:20...

"For where two or three are gathered together in my name, there am I in the midst of them."

The essence of prayer is this. Prayer usually begins with one voice. Then when we reach out to two or even three more believers of like-minded faith something happens in the spiritual realm. God shows up!

Now we know that God will answer that one lone voice without the others. We don't need a vast crowd to draw the presence of God, just one hungry soul can do that.

But let's add to that thought this spiritual principle as well...

Lev. 26:8 ... *"And five of you shall chase an hundred, and an hundred of you shall put ten thousand to flight: and your enemies shall fall before you by the sword."*

Deut. 32:30 ... KJV *"How should one chase a thousand, and two put ten thousand to flight, except their Rock had sold them, and the LORD had shut them up?"*

Like the old song says, "God and I make a majority!" But here's the Barry Manilow moment I want you to have. When our one voice joins the prayers of others and we agree, our power is magnified exponentially. That means it just takes just a few of us to shake heaven and earth if we pray together in faith!

PRAYER GOES FROM A SOLO TO A SYMPHONY!

Definition of Symphony ...

- *an elaborate instrumental composition in three or more movements, similar in form to a sonata but written for an orchestra and usually of far grander proportions and more varied elements.*
- *a concert performed by a symphony orchestra.*
- *anything characterized by a harmonious combination of elements, especially an effective combination of colors.*
- *harmony of sounds.*

My definition ... A bunch of different musicians playing a bunch of different instruments in perfect melody, harmony, and tempo. Each has a different part to play so that the whole song will be complete and beautiful.

SPECIFICALLY ...

In a modern symphony orchestra, there are ... 5 types of stringed instruments, 16 types of wood-wind instruments, 6 types of brass instruments, and no less than 11 types of percussion instruments for a total of 39 different instruments. That also usually means there is an average of 80 musicians all playing from the same score, playing their own part at the appropriate time and tempo.

So, how do all these instruments and musicians come together in perfect pitch and rhythm. Believe it or not it all begins with the Oboe! Most people don't even know what an Oboe is. But the Oboe looks something like a clarinet, but it's sound is unique. In fact, before a symphony orchestra can play, it's the Oboe that tunes every instrument including the dominate bank of violins, cellos, and basses.

Once that is accomplished then the Conductor comes out and stands before the whole orchestra and they begin to play under his direction. What a beautiful illustration of what happens when One voice in prayer, ... joins another, ... then another, until our Conductor arrives and blends them all together to produce physical and spiritual victory, healing, deliverance, and salvation!

THANK YOU, JESUS & MR. MANILOW!

HERE'S THE KICKER ...

In our text, Matt. 18:19, the word "agree" in the original Greek is *symphōneō*. Look familiar? Yep, it's where we get our English word "symphony"! When we pray together, we are part of a body made of different shapes and sizes, different genders, different countries and cultures, all playing from the same score under the direction of ONE Conductor!

Find somebody to pray with! Your prayers may be powerful all by themselves, but with a symphony and the Conductor present anything can happen!

Rev. 8:3-5 ... (3) *"And another angel came and stood at the altar, having a golden censer; and there was given unto him much incense, that he should offer it with the prayers of all saints upon the golden altar which was before the throne.*

(4) And the smoke of the incense, which came with the prayers of the saints, ascended up before God out of the angel's hand.

(5) And the angel took the censer, and filled it with fire of the altar, and cast it into the earth: and there were voices, and thunderings, and lightnings, and an earthquake."

Epilogue

I have reluctantly come to the conclusion that I am more ignorant of the things concerning prayer now than when this journey began many years ago. I believe the depths and the riches of prayer have yet to be plumbed and explored. I also believe that even the great pioneers of prayer were somewhat limited in the fullness of their understanding.

And yet I am confident for those individuals who dedicate and commit themselves to prayer that God has prepared a place in His presence that is beyond our human understanding or experience.

Yes, I believe that there is a supernatural experience in prayer where you literally can clearly and confidently hear the voice of the Almighty Creator. I think He waits with great anticipation for those who are willing to walk that path!

God bless, David L. Martin

Acknowledgements

Joe & Jan McDaniel / BookCrafters

Kari Rios / Graphic Design of Cover

Book Reviewers

Pastor Jimmy Toney

Pastor Steve Waldron

Bishop Randy Adams

Philip Hawley

Rob Caniff

Tim Underwood

CPSIA information can be obtained
at www.ICGtesting.com
Printed in the USA
LVHW080532050623
748254LV00006B/11